Phras

CW00631425

SPANISH

With menu decoder, survival guide and two-way dictionary

Thomas Cook
Publishing

www.thomascookpublishing.com

Introduction......................5

Greetings...........................9

Eating out.........................13

Shopping...........................29

Getting around................37

Accommodation................43

Survival guide..................49

Emergencies..................59

Dictionary.......................63

Quick reference..............95

How to use this guide

The ten chapters in this guide are colour-coded to help you find what you're looking for. These colours are used on the tabs of the pages and in the contents on the opposite page and above.

For quick reference, you'll find some basic expressions on the inside front cover and essential emergency phrases on the inside back cover. There is also a handy reference section for numbers, measurements and clothes sizes at the back of the guide.

Front cover photography © www.photolibrary.com
Cover design/artwork by Sharon Edwards
Photo credits: Andrew Smith (p5 & p29), José A. Warletta (p9), Robson
Oliveira (p32), Chrissi Nerantzi (p46), Elvis Santana (p59) and László
Harri Németh (p63).

Produced by The Content Works Ltd.
www.thecontentworks.com
Design concept: Mike Wade
Layout: Tika Stefano
Text: Nina Brixa
Editing: Begoña Juarros & Amanda Castleman
Proofing: Wendy Janes
Project editor: Begoña Juarros
Management: Lisa Plumridge & Rik Mulder

Published by Thomas Cook Publishing
A division of Thomas Cook Tour Operations Limited
PO Box 227, Unit 18, Coningsby Road
Peterborough PE3 8SB, United Kingdom
Company Registration N° 1450464 England
email: books@thomascook.com
www.thomascookpublishing.com
+ 44 (0)1733 416477

ISBN-13: 978-184157-678-7

First edition © 2007 Thomas Cook Publishing
Text © 2007 Thomas Cook Publishing

Project Editor: Kelly Pipes
Production/DTP: Steven Collins

Printed and bound in Italy by Printer Trento

Introduction

Spain is a land of boundless energy; its history rich with artists, explorers and empire-builders. Unsurprisingly, this dynamic nation spread its culture far and wide. The mother tongue of 400 million people, Spanish is the world's fourth most common language, after Chinese, Hindi and English.

Memorising even a few phrases will greatly improve your travel experience. Simple statements – like **por favor** (please) and **muchas gracias** (thank you) – demonstrate good intentions, which carry a lot of weight in such a proud, courteous society. So don't be shy: ¡**hable Español!**

The basics

Spanish is descended from Latin, like French and Italian. However, it's spiced with Arabic, thanks to 700 years of Moorish influence. Place-names – Guadarrama, Benidorm and Benicassim, for example – and words like **alhaja** (jewel) and **ajedrez** (chess) reflect these roots.

The melting pot influences all Spain's languages. Catalan somewhat resembles a mix of French and Spanish, while Galician sounds vaguely Portuguese. Basque, the tricky tongue of the Pyrenees, has no Latin or Indo-European base. Experts suggest wild theories, including links with the Eskimos or the Ainu, the aboriginal inhabitants of Japan. This book concentrates on Castilian, the dominant and official tongue.

Even among Castilian Spanish-speakers, accents vary. Foreigners generally understand northerners more easily; the southern style – in its fast pace and pronunciation – is closer to

False friends

English and Spanish have quite a few similar terms. Sometimes it's even possible to guess a term by adding "o" or "a".

Occasionally that tactic goes horribly, horribly wrong. Here are some "false friends": words that resemble each other, but express very different ideas:

Embarazada – pregnant (not embarrassed)

Sensible – sensitive (not sensible)

Constipada – to have a cold (not to be constipated)

Simpático – friendly (not sympathetic)

Petróleo – oil (not petrol)

Librería – bookshop (not a library)

those in Latin America and the Canary Islands. For example, they lisp the letters "c" and "z" into a "th" sound – Barthelona being a familiar example – and strengthen the "s". The polite form of "you," **usted**, also features in these areas, instead of **tú**.

Grammar

Spanish is a very phonetic language: you say what you see – a real boon for beginners.

Nouns fall into three groups: masculine (**el vino**), feminine (**la cerveza**) or neutral (**lo bueno**). Generally, but not always, masculine words end in "o" and feminine in "a". To talk about more than one object, add "s" to words that conclude with a vowel and "es" after a consonant.

Words flow in an order similar to English, but adjectives tend to come after the words they describe: for example, **comida buena** versus "good food".

Spanish marks a question or exclamation before and after the phrase – that distinctive mirrored punctuation:

¿Qué tal?   **¡Hola!**

Also, the ending of a verb indicates who is doing the action and when; **deseo** means "I wish", while **deseamos** is "we wish". A casual visitor doesn't need to memorize all the possibilities, just understand why a word can change from phrase to phrase.

Here's the most basic way to express an idea happening now. Take the infinitive – the "to do" form listed in a dictionary – and lop off the last two letters:

dese-ar **com-er** **part-ir**
to wish   to eat   to leave

Now add the appropriate ending:

yo	**dese-o**	**com-o**	**part-o**
I	wish	eat	leave

tú	**dese-as**	**com-es**	**part-es**
You	wish	eat	leave

él, ella He/She	dese-a wishes	com-e eats	part-e leaves
nos We	**dese-amos** wish	**com-emos** eat	**part-imos** leave
vos You	**dese-áis** wish	**com-éis** eat	**part-ís** leave
ellos, ellas They	**dese-an** wish	**com-en** eat	**part-en** leave

Most importantly, don't let the grammar scare you. Yes, Spanish is an intricate, nuanced language, the tongue of Cervantes and other great poets. But it's also a very forgiving and user-friendly one at a basic level. And locals appreciate any attempt, especially when it's paired with a wide smile.

Basic conversation

Yes	**Sí**	*see*
No	**No**	*no*
Please	**Por favor**	*por fabor*
Thank you	**Gracias**	*grathyas*
You're welcome	**De nada**	*de nada*
Sorry	**Perdón**	*perdon*
Excuse me (apology)	**Lo siento**	*lo syento*
Excuse me (to get attention)	**Perdone**	*perdoneh*
Do you speak English?	**¿Habla inglés?**	*abla eengles?*
I don't speak Spanish	**No hablo español**	*no ablo espanyol*
I speak a little Spanish	**Hablo un poco de español**	*ablo oon poko de espanyol*
What?	**¿Cómo dice?**	*komo deethe?*
I understand	**Entiendo**	*entyendo*
I don't understand	**No entiendo**	*no entyendo*
Do you understand?	**¿Entiende?**	*entyende?*
I don't know	**No sé**	*no seh*
Can you... please?	**¿Puede... por favor?**	*pwede... por fabor?*
- speak more slowly	**- hablar más despacio**	*ablar mas despathyo?*
- repeat that	**- repetirlo**	*repeteerlo?*

8

Greetings

Try to speak some Spanish and you'll earn an even friendlier welcome in this warm-blooded country. Although many locals – especially in the coastal areas – are happy to practise English, they will appreciate your efforts to speak their language. Beware, though, that regional accent variations can be extreme. Just like the country itself, really. The sultry south has more joie de vivre: it's the land of flamenco and bullfighting. Go north for greener scenery, mountains, wholesome food and a slightly more serious attitude.

Meeting someone

Hello	**Hola**	_o_lah
Hi	**Hola**	_o_lah
Good morning	**Buenos días**	bw_e_nos d_ee_as
Good afternoon	**Buenas tardes**	bw_e_nas _tar_des
Good evening	**Buenas tardes**	bw_e_nas _tar_des
Sir/Mr	**Señor/Sr**	seny_or_/seny_or_
Madam/Mrs	**Señora/Sra**	seny_o_ra/seny_o_ra
Miss	**Señorita**	seny_oreeta_
How are you?	**¿Cómo está?**	_ko_mo est_a_?
Fine, thank you	**Bien, gracias**	by_e_n, _gra_thyas
And you?	**¿Y usted?**	ee oost_ed_?
Very well	**Muy bien**	mooy by_e_n
Not very well	**No muy bien**	no mooy by_e_n

Make some noise!

Spaniards love to be in large, boisterous crowds, and the noise levels in bars (the **ambiente**) can be deafening. Join in and have fun!

Small talk

My name is...	**Me llamo...**	me _ya_mo...
What's your name?	**¿Cómo se llama?**	_ko_mo se _ya_ma?
I'm pleased to meet you	**Encantado(a) de conocerle(a)**	enkant_a_do(a) de konother_le(a)
Where are you from?	**¿De dónde es?**	de _dond_eh es?
I am from Britain	**Soy de Gran Bretaña**	soy de gran bretany
Do you live here?	**¿Vive aquí?**	_bee_be ak_ee_?

This is a great...	Este/a es... estupendo(a)	*este/es... estoopen-do(a)*
- country	- un país	- *oon pays*
- city/town	- una ciudad	- *oona theewdad*
I am staying at...	Me hospedo en...	*me ospedo en...*

I'm just here for the day	Estoy aquí sólo para pasar el día	*estoy akee solo para pasar el deea*
I'm in ... for	Estoy en... por	*estoy akee por...*
- a weekend	- un fin de semana	- *oon feen de semana*
- a week	- una semana	- *oona semana*

| How old are you? | ¿Cuántos años tiene? | *kwantos anyos tyene?* |
| I'm... years old | Tengo... años | *tengo...anyos* |

Family

This is my...	Este(a) es mi...	*este(a) es mee...*
- husband	- esposo	- *esposo*
- wife	- esposa	- *esposa*
- partner	- pareja	- *pareha*
- boyfriend/ girlfriend	- novio/novia	- *nobyo/nobya*

I have a...	Tengo un(a)...	*tengo oon(a)...*
- son	- hijo	- *eeho*
- daughter	- hija	- *eeha*
- grandson	- nieto	- *nyeto*
- granddaughter	- nieta	- *nyeta*

Do you have...	¿Tiene...	*tyene...*
- children?	- hijos?	- *eehos?*
- grandchildren?	- nietos?	- *nyetos?*
I don't have children	No tengo hijos	- *no tengo eehos*

Are you married?	¿Está casado/a?	*esta kasado/a?*
I'm...	Estoy...	*estoy...*
- single	- soltero/a	- *soltero/a*
- married	- casado/a	- *kasado/a*
- divorced	- divorciado/a	- *deeborthyado/a*
- a widow/widower	- viudo/viuda	- *byoodo/byooda*

Mum's the word

For Spaniards, family goes above everything. Never speak badly about a man's mother or a mother's child, unless you're spoiling for trouble.

Saying goodbye

Goodbye	**Adiós**	_adyos_
Good night	**Buenas noches**	_bwenas noches_
Sleep well	**Que duerma bien**	_keh dwerma byen_
See you later	**Hasta luego**	_asta lwego_
Have a good trip	**Buen viaje**	_bwen byahe_
It was nice meeting you	**Ha sido un placer conocerle(a)**	_a seedo oon plather konotherle(a)_
All the best	**Que vaya todo bien**	_ke baya todo byen_
Have fun	**Páselo bien**	_paselo byen_
Good luck	**Buena suerte**	_bwena swerte_
Keep in touch	**Manténgase en contacto**	_mantengase en kontakto_
My address is...	**Mi dirección es...**	_mee deerekthyon es..._
What's your...	**¿Cuál es su...**	_kwal es soo..._
- address?	**- dirección?**	_- deerekthyon?_
- email?	**- correo electrónico?**	_- korreo elektroneeko?_
- telephone number?	**- número de teléfono?**	_- noomero de telephono?_

Eating out

"Late" and "meaty" were the classic complaints about Spanish cuisine. But a new sensitivity has emerged, both in chefs' preparations and tourists' appreciation. The country, after all, has much to offer: superb beef, pork and game, sun-ripened crops and grapevines, and seafood fresh from the Atlantic and Mediterranean.

Menu favourites include **tapas**, **jamón** and **paella**. Yet each region fiercely defends its culinary style, favourite ingredients and signature dishes. This makes travel here a true gastronomic voyage, from the **gazpacho** of Andalusia to the hotpots of the Canaries via **arroz negro**, the squid-ink risotto of the north.

¡Buen provecho!

13

Introduction

Food is supremely important in Spanish culture. Most social time is spent eating: coffee mid-morning with **churros** (fried dough bars); early-afternoon **aperitivo** with **tapas**; a mid-afternoon lunch usually the main meal of the day with three courses; then **tapas** again early evening; and finally a late, but light, dinner.

I'd like...	**Quisiera...**	*keesyera...*
- a table for two	**- una mesa para dos**	*- oona mesa para dos*
- a sandwich	**- un bocadillo**	*- oon bokadeeyo*
- a coffee	**- un café**	*- oon kapheh*
- a tea (with milk)	**- un té (con leche)**	*- oon teh (kon leche)*
Do you have a menu in English?	**¿Tiene un menú en inglés?**	*tyene oon menoo en eengles?*
The bill, please	**La cuenta, por favor**	*la kwenta, por fabor*

You may hear...

¿Fumadores o no fumadores?	*phoomadores o no phoomadores?*	Smoking or non-smoking?
¿Qué va a tomar?	*keh va a tomar?*	What are you going to have?

The cuisines of Spain

Tapas

Talk of Spanish food and most people think "tapas". The appetizers originated in Andalusia, but every region now has its own specialities. **Tapas** fall into three categories: **pincho** (bite size), **tapa** (snack) and **ración** (plateful). Don't let the waiter talk you into **raciones**: variety is the point. Following are some popular items, but please see the Menu decoder for more (p.21).

Almejas	*almehas*	Clams
Anchoas fritas	*anchoas phreetas*	Deep-fried anchovies
Callos	*kayos*	Tripe
Caracoles	*karakoles*	Snails, usually in paprika sauce
Gambas a la plancha	*gambas a la plancha*	Grilled shrimps

Madrid & central Spain

The cuisine in central Spain is as old as its castles. Expect wood-roasted meats, hearty stews and soups, often eaten cold. Madrid, on the other hand, is trendier – most recently falling for minimalist fusion fare. International restaurants are also adding spice, as Japanese, Middle Eastern and Latin American establishments join the usual suspects like Italian and Chinese.

Dinner time or sleep time?

Spanish restaurants typically fill between 10pm and midnight, much to some visitors' alarm. Impatient eaters should patch together a meal from **tapas**. Street snacks include **churros** (deep-fried dough) and **bocadillos** (baguette-style sandwiches).

Signature dishes

(see the Menu decoder for more dishes)

Cocido madrileño	*kotheedo madreelenyo*	Pork, vegetable and chickpeas stew
Salmorejo	*salmoreho*	Thick cold tomato soup
Dorada a la sal	*dorada a la sal*	Salt-baked sea bream
Emperador con tomate	*emperador kon tomate*	Swordfish in tomato sauce
Patatas bravas	*patatas brabas*	Potatoes in spicy tomato sauce

Eastern Spain & the Mediterranean coast

Paella is known the world over as Spain's signature dish, but Valencians justifiably lay claim to this concoction of rice, meat and poultry. Catalan cooking has a long and fishy tradition, while Barcelona's restaurant scene rivals the capital's.

Signature dishes
(see the Menu decoder for more dishes)

Paella valenciana	*paeya balentheeana*	Rice with rabbit and chicken, and sometimes eel
Arroz negro	*arroth negro*	Rice with squid ink sauce
Fideuá de marisco	*pheedeooa de mareesko*	Fine pasta noodles with seafood
Tumbet	*toombeh*	Aubergine, tomatoes, peppers and potatoes cooked in an earthenware pot
Cassolada	*kasolada*	Pork and vegetable stew

Beyond Rioja and sherry

Spain is justifiably famous for red Riojas and sherry (fortified wine), but its **bodegas** (wine shops) have more in store, from crisp Galician whites to Catalonian cavas, the "Spanish champagne".

Southern Spain

Almond and honey pastries, and **granizados** (iced drinks) reveal the South's Moorish past. Andalusia is also the birthplace of the cold **gazpacho** soup and **pescadito frito** (fried fish). Its famous white villages are good places to try the superb **ibérico** ham.

Signature dishes
(see the Menu decoder for more dishes)

Pescadito frito	*peskadeeto phreeto*	Mixed fried fish
Chanquetes	*chanketes*	Whitebait
Gazpacho	*gathpacho*	Cold cucumber, tomato soup

Cazón en adobo	*kathon en adobo*	Marinated dogfish
Patatas arrugadas	*patatas arroogadas*	Potatoes cooked in their skins

The king of hams

Pigs grow fat on acorns and chestnuts, giving Spain's celebrated **jamón ibérico** a nutty flavour. The best of these cured hams come from Andalusia and neighbouring Extremadura.

Northern Spain

Live to eat, rather than eat to live, in the north of Spain. Basques take dining out seriously. San Sebastián and Bilbao, in particular, have many top-class restaurants. Asturias is famed for cheese and cider, Galicia has an abundance of seafood, but also superb beef.

Signature dishes

(see the Menu decoder for more dishes)

Bacalao al pil-pil	*bakalao al peel-peel*	Cod in garlic and olive oil sauce
Marmitako	*marmeetako*	Tuna and potato stew
Caldeirada	*kaldeyrada*	Fish soup
Vieiras de Santiago	*byeras de santyago*	Shelled scallops in a brandy sauce
Fabada asturiana	*fabada astooryana*	Pork and butter bean stew

The Balearic & Canary Islands

Each island has a distinct flavour – and specialities to match: **cuina mallorquina** (Mallorcan cuisine) is mainly pork based, while Menorca is lobster country. In the Canaries, **gofio** (flour made from toasted wheat or maize) stars in many traditional recipes.

Signature dishes
(see the Menu decoder for more dishes)

Caldereta de langosta	*kaldereta de langosta*	Spicy lobster stew
Ensaimada	*ensaymada*	Spiral sugar-dusted pastry
Conejo al salmorejo	*koneho al salmoreho*	Rabbit marinated in oil and herbs
Puchero canario	*poochero kanaryo*	Hotpot
Sancocho	*sankocho*	Fish and vegetable stew

Wine, beer & spirits

Spaniards sip both beer and wine with **tapas**, but formal meals merit a bottle. La Rioja, in the north, produces the country's best red vintages. The scorching summers of Jerez produce sweet, fat grapes – the basis of the south's world-famous sherries.

I'd like to try...	**Quisiera probar...**	*keesyera probar...*
- red wine punch	**- sangría**	*- sangreea*
- coffee with brandy	**- un carajillo**	*- oon karaheeyo*
- dry sherry	**- un fino**	*- oon feeno*
- sweet alcoholic digestive	**- un pacharán**	*- oon pacharan*
- wine from the Rioja region	**- un rioja**	*- oon reeoha*

The New World
Conquistadores introduced many staple foods to Europe. Tomatoes, peppers and even potatoes originate from the Americas. Spaniards quickly adopted these new ingredients, while it took several hundred years for Italians to accept that tomatoes weren't poisonous.

Could I have...	¿Me pone...	me _pone_...
- a beer?	- una cerveza?	- _oo_na ther_beth_a?
- a glass/a bottle of white/red/rosé wine?	- un vaso/una botella de vino blanco/tinto/ros-ado?	- oon _baso_/_oo_na bo_tey_a de _beeno_ _blanko_/_teento_/rosa-do?
- a glass/a bottle of cava	- una copa/una botella de cava?	- _oo_na _kopa_/_oo_na bo_tella_ de cava?
- a gin and tonic?	- un gin tonic?	- oon heen _toneek_?
- a rum and coke?	- un cubata?	- oon koo_bata_?
- a whisky?	- un güisqui?	- oon _beeskee_?

Matrimonio Murcians "marry" two kinds of anchovies: one salty, the other pickled in vinegar. The union is considered a delicacy.

You may hear...

¿Qué le pongo?	keh le _pongo_?	What can I get you?
¿Cómo lo quiere?	_komo_ lo _kyere_?	How would you like it?
¿Con o sin hielo?	kon o seen _yelo_?	With or without ice?
¿Frío/a o natural?	_freeo_/a o natoo_ral_?	Cold or room temperature?

Snacks & refreshments

Spain has a rich café culture: linger on a **terraza** (terrace) with a small fierce coffee – perhaps even a **carajillo** (brandy-spiked espresso). Many bars serve snacks ranging from **bocadillos** (baguette-style sandwiches) to **raciones** (light meals). Leave a few coins as a tip.

Chocolate con churros	choko_late_ kon _choorros_	Hot chocolate and fritters for dipping
Calamares	kala_mares_	Deep-fried squid
Aceitunas	athey_too_nas	Olives
Café con hielo	ka_pheh_ kon _hielo_	Iced black coffee

| Horchata | *orchata* | Milky drink with nuts |
| Granizado | *graneethado* | Crushed ice drink |

Vegetarians & special requirements

I'm vegetarian	**Soy vegetariano/a**	*soy behetaryano/a*
I don't eat...	**No como...**	*no komo...*
- meat	**- carne**	*- karne*
- fish	**- pescado**	*- peskado*

| Could you cook something without meat in it? | **¿Me pueden preparar algo sin carne?** | *me pweden preparar algo seen karne?* |

What's in this?	**¿Qué lleva esto?**	*keh yeba esto?*
I'm allergic to...	**Tengo alergia a...**	*tengo alerhya a...*
- to nuts	**- a los frutos secos**	*- a los phrootos sekos*
- to gluten	**-al gluten**	*- al glooten*
- to dairy	**- a los productos lácteos**	*- a los prodooktos lakteos*

Children

Are children welcome?	**¿Admiten niños?**	*admeeten neenyos?*
Do you have a children's menu?	**¿Tienen menú para niños?**	*tyenen menoo para neenyos?*
What dishes are good for children?	**¿Qué platos son buenos para niños?**	*keh platos son bwenos para neenyos?*

Oil for food

Maybe it's the Moorish-Arab influence, but Spain remains the world's largest oil producer – olive oil, that is. A splash enlivens most dishes, down to the quintessential **pan con tomate** (toast rubbed with tomato and drizzled with olive oil).

Essentials

Breakfast	**El desayuno**	*el desayoono*
Lunch	**La comida/el almuerzo**	*la komeeda/el almooertho*
Dinner	**La cena**	*le thena*
Cover charge	**El cubierto**	*el koobyerto*
VAT inclusive	**IVA incluido**	*eeba eenklooeedo*
Service included	**Servicio incluido**	*serbeetheeo eenklooeedo*
Credit cards (not) accepted	**(no) aceptamos tarjetas de crédito**	*(no) atheptamos tarhettas de kredeeto*
First course	**El primer plato**	*el preemer plato*
Second course	**El segundo plato**	*el segoondo plato*
Dessert	**El postre**	*el postre*
Dish of the day	**El plato del día**	*el plato del deea*
House specials	**Las especialidades de la casa**	*las espetheealeedades de la kasa*
Set menu	**El menú del día**	*el menoo del deea*
A la carte menu	**El menú a la carta**	*el menoo a la karta*
Tourist menu	**El menú turista**	*el menoo tooreesta*
Wine list	**La carta de vinos**	*la karta de beenos*
Drinks menu	**El menú de bebidas**	*el menoo de bebeedas*
Snack menu	**El menú de tapas**	*el menoo de tapas*

Methods of preparation

Baked	**Al horno**	*al orno*
Boiled	**Cocido/a**	*kotheedo/a*
Braised	**Cocido/a a fuego lento**	*kotheedo/a a phooego lento*
Breaded	**Rebozado/a**	*rebothado/a*
Deep-fried	**Frito/a en mucho aceite**	*phreeto/a en moocho atheyte*
Fresh	**Fresco/a**	*phresko/a*
Fried	**Frito/a**	*phreeto/a*
Frozen	**Congelado/a**	*konhelado/a*
Grilled/broiled	**Al gril/A la parrilla**	*al greel/ a la pareeya*

Albigonthingy?

Don't bother to memorise the names of desirable tapas dishes. Usually the selection is displayed behind the counter – just point out your picks. Start with a glass of sherry for an authentic experience.

Sautéed	**Salteado/a**	salteado/a
Smoked	**Ahumado/a**	aoo*ma*do/a
Spicy (flavour)	**Especiado/a**	espe*theea*do/a
Spicy (hot)	**Picante**	pee*kan*te
Steamed	**Al vapor**	al ba*por*
Stewed	**Estofado/a**	esto*pha*do/a
Stuffed	**Relleno/a**	re*ye*no/a
Sweet	**Dulce**	*dool*the
Rare	**Poco hecho/a**	*po*ko *e*cho/a
Medium	**Normal**	nor*mal*
Well done	**Bien hecho/a**	byen *e*cho/a

Common food items

Beef	**La carne de vaca**	la *kar*ne de *ba*ka
Chicken	**El pollo**	el *po*yo
Turkey	**El pavo**	el *pa*bo
Lamb	**El cordero**	el kor*de*ro

Pork	**La carne de cerdo**	*la karne de therdo*
Rabbit	**El conejo**	*el koneho*
Fish	**El pescado**	*el peskado*
Seafood	**El marisco**	*el mareesko*
Tuna	**El atún**	*el atoon*
Beans	**Las judías**	*las hoodeeas*
Cheese	**El queso**	*el keso*
Eggs	**Los huevos**	*los ooebos*
Lentils	**Las lentejas**	*las lentehas*
Pasta/noodles	**La pasta/los fideos**	*la pasta/los pheedeos*
Rice	**El arroz**	*el arroth*
Cabbage	**La berza**	*la bertha*
Carrots	**Las zanahorias**	*las thanaoreeas*
Cucumber	**El pepino**	*el pepeeno*
Garlic	**El ajo**	*el aho*
Mushrooms	**Los champiñones**	*los champeenyones*
Olives	**Las aceitunas/las olives**	*las atheytoonas/las oleebes*
Onion	**La cebolla**	*la theboya*
Potato	**La patata**	*la patata*
Red/green pepper	**El pimiento rojo/verde**	*el peemyento roho/berde*
Tomato	**El tomate**	*el tomate*
Vegetables	**Las verduras**	*las berdooras*
Bread	**El pan**	*el pan*
Oil	**El aceite**	*el atheyte*
Pepper	**La pimienta**	*la peemyenta*
Salt	**La sal**	*la sal*
Vinegar	**El vinagre**	*el beenagre*
Cake	**El pastel**	*el pastel*
Cereal	**Los cereales**	*los thereales*
Cream	**La nata**	*la nata*
Fruit	**La fruta**	*la phroota*
Ice-cream	**El helado**	*el elado*
Milk	**La leche**	*la leche*
Tart	**La tarta**	*la tarta*

Popular sauces

Ali-oli	_alee-olee_	Olive oil and garlic creamy sauce
Chilindrón	_cheeleendron_	Pepper, tomatoes, fried onions and meat sauce
Mojo	_moho_	Olive oil, vinegar, garlic and spices sauce
Salsa de tomate	_salsa de tomate_	Tomato sauce
Salsa romesco	_salsa romesko_	Almonds, hazelnuts and chilli sauce
Salsa verde	_salsa berde_	Parsley and olive oil sauce
Sofrito	_sophreeto_	Onions, garlic and tomato sauce

Hot 'n' spicy

Spanish cuisine can be spicy, but is seldom hot. For a burn-buzz, order **patatas bravas**: fried potatoes in a hot tomato sauce. **Chorizo** – paprika-laced sausage – comes in two varieties: **picante** (hot) and **dulce** (sweet).

Tapas

Albóndigas con tomate	_albondeegas kon tomate_	Meatballs in tomato sauce
Boquerones en vinagre	_boquerones en beenagre_	Marinated fresh anchovies
Chanquetes	_chanketes_	Whitebait
Chorizo al vino	_choreetho al beeno_	Spicy sausage cooked in wine
Croquetas	_kroketas_	Meat or fish croquettes
Gambas al ajillo	_gambas al aheeyo_	Prawns in garlic sauce

Patatas bravas	*patatas brabas*	Fried potatoes in spicy tomato sauce
Pulpo a la gallega	*poolpo a la gayega*	Marinated octopus
Tortilla de patata	*torteeya de patata*	Spanish omelette

First course dishes

Alcachofas con jamón	*alkachophas kon hamon*	Sautéed artichokes with cured ham
Alubias	*aloobyas*	Bean stew
Arroz a la cubana	*arroth a la koobana*	Rice with a fried egg in a tomato sauce
Cazuela de fideos	*kathooela de pheedeos*	Beans, meat and noodle stew
Chanfaina	*chanphayna*	Pork stew
Cóctel de gambas	*koktel de gambas*	Prawn cocktail
Consomé	*konsomeh*	Chicken broth sometimes served with egg yolk
Crema de espárragos	*krema de esparragos*	Asparagus cream
Ensalada mixta	*ensalada mista*	Lettuce, tomatoes, tuna, boiled egg and onion salad
Ensaladilla rusa	*ensaladeeya roosa*	Vegetable salad with boiled eggs and tuna in mayonnaise
Escalivada	*eskaleebada*	Char-grilled vegetable salad
Espárragos con mayonesa	*esparragos kon mayonesa*	Asparagus served with mayonnaise
Estofado de ternera	*estophado de ternera*	Veal stew
Gazpacho	*gathpacho*	Cold vegetable soup
Menestra de verduras	*menestra de berdooras*	Boiled vegetables with ham
Paella de marisco	*paeya de mareesko*	Rice and seafood paella
Sopa de pescado	*sopa de peskado*	Fish soup

Second course dishes

Bacalao al ajo arriero	*bacalao al aho arryero*	Fried salt cod with a garlic, vinegar, paprika and parsley sauce
Cabrito al horno	*kabreeto al orno*	Roast kid
Calamares en su tinta	*kalamares en soo teenta*	Squid served with squid (black) sauce
Caldereta de pescado	*kaldereta de peskado*	Fish stew
Chuletillas de cordero	*chooleteeyas de kordero*	Fried lamb chops
Churrasco	*choorasko*	Barbecued steak
Cochinillo asado	*kocheeneeyo asado*	Roast piglet
Cordero asado	*kordero asado*	Roast lamb
Dorada al horno	*dorada al orno*	Baked sea bream
Entrecot a la plancha	*entrekot a la plancha*	Grilled boneless beef steak
Filete de ternera	*pheelete de ternera*	Veal steak
Lubina al horno	*loobeena al orno*	Baked sea bass
Merluza a la romana	*merlootha a la romana*	Fried hake in batter
Parillada de pescado	*pareeyada de peskado*	Mixed fish grill
Pimientos rellenos	*peemyentos reyenos*	Stuffed red peppers (with fish or meat)
Solomillo de ternera	*solomeeyo de ternera*	Veal sirloin
Trucha a la navarra	*troocha a la nabarra*	Trout with cured ham stuffing

Side dishes

Patatas fritas	*patatas phreetas*	Chips
Puré de patatas	*pooreh de patatas*	Mashed potatoes
Guarnición	*gwarneethyon*	Vegetables
Ensalada	*ensalada*	Salad

Desserts

Arroz con leche	*arroth kon leche*	Rice pudding with cinnamon
Crema catalana	*krema katalana*	Custard topped with caramelised sugar

Chocolate con churros

The street snacks of choice are dough bars dunked in thick hot chocolate or sprinkled with sugar. After a long night out, this sweet mix of grease and carbohydrates becomes especially appealing.

Cuajada	*kwahada*	Similar to natural yogurt served with honey or sugar
Flan	*flan*	Crème caramel
Fruta del tiempo	*phroota del tyempo*	Fruit of the season
Helados variados	*elados bareeados*	Ice-cream (several flavours)
Macedonia de fruta	*mathedonya de phroota*	Fruit salad
Natillas	*natiyas*	Custard flavoured with cinnamon
Sorbete de limón	*sorbete de leemon*	Lemon sorbet
Tabla de quesos	*tabla de kesos*	Cheese platter
Tarta de manzana	*tarta de manthana*	Apple tart
Tarta de queso	*tarta de keso*	Cheesecake

Drinks

Café con leche	*kapheh kon leche*	Coffee with milk
Café solo	*kapheh solo*	Black coffee
Carajillo	*karaheeyo*	Black coffee with brandy
Chocolate	*chokolatte*	Thick hot chocolate
Cortado	*kortado*	Strong coffee with a shot of milk

Descafeinado (con leche)	deskapheynado (kon leche)	Decaffeinated coffee (with milk)
Infusión	eenphoosyon	Herbal tea
Té (con leche/limón)	te (kon leche/leemon)	Tea (with milk/lemon)
Agua mineral sin/con gas	agwa meeneral seen/kon gas	Mineral water, still/sparkling
Blanco y negro	blanko ee negro	Milky coffee with ice
Café con hielo	kapheh kon yelo	Black iced coffee
Cerveza / cerveza de barril	therbetha / therbetha de barreel	Beer/Draught beer
Coca-cola	koka-kola	Coke
Refrescos	rephreskos	Soft drinks
Vino blanco/tinto/ rosado	beeno blanko/ teento/rosado	White/red/ rosé wine
Zumo de naranja	thoomo de naranha	Orange juice
Zumo de tomate	thoomo de tomate	Tomato juice

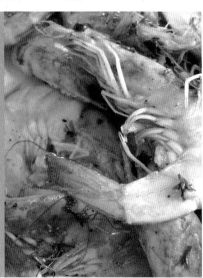

A mecca for seafood lovers

Poised between the Atlantic and Mediterranean, Spain has a range of fresh and fine seafood: from paella to **zarzuela** (stew) and garlic prawns to **bacalao** (cod).

Shopping

Small, family-run businesses still prevail in Spain, which makes each shopping trip a cultural excursion. Most boutiques open around 10am and close for siesta, as well as Saturday afternoons and Mondays.

Arts and crafts have a long tradition here: expect precious handmade items, such as pottery, ceramics, woodwork, embroidery and lace, and silver and gold jewellery. Spanish leather goods are renowned and remain reasonably priced.

Madrid and Barcelona both have a wide range of international boutiques and upmarket shopping malls. A visit to El Rastro, the capital's antique and flea market, is highly recommended for Sunday mornings, when other sights are closed.

Essentials

English	Spanish	Pronunciation
Where can I buy...?	¿Dónde puedo comprar... ?	*dondeh pwedo komprar...?*
I'd like to buy...	Me gustaría comprar...	*me goostareea komprar...*
Do you have...?	¿Tienen... ?	*tyenen...?*
Do you sell...?	¿Venden... ?	*benden...?*
I'd like this	Quiero esto	*kyero esto*
I'd prefer...	Preferiría...	*prephereereea...*
Could you show me...?	¿Me podría enseñar... ?	*me podreea ensenyar...?*
I'm just looking, thanks	Sólo estoy mirando, gracias	*solo estoy meerando, grathyas*
How much is it?	¿Cuánto cuesta?	*kwanto kwesta?*
Could you write down the price?	¿Puede escribir el precio?	*pwede eskreebeer el prethyo?*
Do you have any items on sale?	¿Tienen algo rebajado?	*tyenen algo rebahado?*
Could I have a discount?	¿Me puede hacer un descuento?	*me pwede ather oon deskwento?*
Nothing else, thanks	Nada más, gracias	*nada mas, grathyas*
Do you accept credit cards?	¿Aceptan tarjetas de crédito?	*atheptan tarhettas de kredeeto?*
It's a present, could I have it wrapped, please?	Es un regalo, ¿me lo envuelve por favor?	*es oon regalo, me lo embwelbe por phabor?*
Could you post it to...?	¿Lo pueden enviar a... ?	*lo pweden enbyar a...?*
Can I exchange it?	¿Puedo cambiarlo?	*pwedo kambyarlo?*
I'd like to return this	Quisiera devolver esto	*keesyera debolber esto*
Can I have a refund?	¿Me puede devolver el dinero?	*me pwede debolber el deenero*

Local specialities

Great regional souvenirs include handmade fans or shawls from Valencia, a bottle of Rioja or sherry, and silver filigree jewellery from Andalusia. Or splash out on metal handiwork in towns such as Toledo and Albacete. Skip the porcelain tortilla stand, however; unless professionally shipped, it won't travel well.

Can you recommend a shop selling local specialities?	¿Me puede recomendar una tienda de productos típicos de la región?	*me pwede rekomendar oona tyenda de prodooktos teepeekos de la reheeon?*
What are the local specialities?	¿Qué productos son típicos de la región?	*keh prodooktos son teepeekos de la reheeon?*

Cordoban acoustic guitars

A country inflamed by flamenco naturally requires top-notch instruments. The artisans of Córdoba produce guitars that are treasured by the world's finest musicians.

What should I buy from here?	¿Qué me aconseja comprar aquí?	*keh me akonseha komprar akee?*
Is... (leather) good quality?	¿Es de buena calidad... (el cuero)?	*es de bwena kaleedath... (el kooero)?*
Do you make the... (ceramics) yourself?	¿Hace usted... (las cerámicas)?	*athe oosteth... (las therameekas)?*
Is it hand made?	¿Está hecho/a a mano?	*estah echo/a a mano?*
Do you make it to measure?	¿Lo/a hacen a medida?	*lo/a athen a medeeda?*
Can I order one?	¿Me encargan uno/a?	*me enkargan oono/a?*

Popular things to buy

Abanicos	*abaneekos*	Hand-held fans
Botijos	*boteehos*	Spouted drinking pitchers
Cerámica	*therameeka*	Ceramics

Cestería	*thestereea*	Basketwork
Encajes	*enkahes*	Lace
Figuras de Navidad	*pheegooras de nabeedath*	Christmas nativity figures
Figuras de porcelana de Lladró	*pheegooras de porthelana de yadro*	Lladró porcelain figures
Filigrana	*pheeleegrana*	Silver filigree jewellery
Jamón serrano	*hamon serrano*	Cured mountain ham
Jarapas	*harapas*	Cotton rugs
Jerez	*hereth*	Sherry
Mantas de lana	*mantas de lana*	Woollen blankets
Marquetería	*marketereea*	Marquetry (wood inlaid with bone, ivory or wood)
Productos de cuero	*prodooktos de kooero*	Saddlery and leather items
Vino de Rioja	*beeno de reeoha*	Rioja wine

Crianza, Reserva or Gran Reserva?

Spain has more than 50 recognized wine regions, Rioja being the most famous. Tour a winery or simply sample its wares in a **bodega**. A bottle or two also makes an excellent gift to bring home: just be aware of import limits.

Clothes & shoes

Spain has a young and vivid fashion scene. Boutiques sell innovative creations, exclusives on the European market. The narrow alleys of Barcelona's Barrio Gótico are a good hunting ground. For more mainstream styles, Mango and Zara have outlets all over the country. The price level is somewhat lower than in the UK.

Where is the... department?	**¿Dónde está la sección de...**	*dondeh estah la sekthyon de...*

Boots, belts & saddles

Shopping for leather products is a must in Spain: not always cheap but still value for money. Think outside the purse box: designers also sell briefcases, luggage and couture sheepskin coats, for example.

- clothes	**- ropa?**	- _ropa?_
- shoe	**- calzado?**	- _kalthado?_
- women's	**- mujeres?**	- _mooheres?_
- men's	**- hombres?**	- _ombres?_
- children's	**- niños?**	- _neenyos?_
I'm looking for...	**Estoy buscando...**	_estoy booskando..._
- a skirt	**- una falda**	- _oona falda_
- trousers	**- unos pantalones**	- _oonos pantalones_
- a top	**- un top**	- _oon top_
- a jacket	**- una chaqueta**	- _oona chaketta_
- a T-shirt	**- una camiseta**	- _oona kameesetta_
- jeans	**- unos vaqueros**	- _oonos bakeros_
- shoes	**- unos zapatos**	- _oonos thapatos_
- underwear	**- ropa interior**	- _ropa eenteryor_
Can I try it on?	**¿Puedo probármelo/a?**	_pwedo probarmelo/a?_
What size is it?	**¿Qué talla es?**	_keh taya es?_
My size is...	**Uso la talla...**	_uso la taya..._
- small	**- pequeña**	- _pekenya_
- medium	**- mediana**	- _medeeana_
- large	**- grande**	- _grande_

(see clothes size converter on p.96 for full range of sizes)

Do you have this in my size?	**¿Tienen esto en mi talla?**	_tyenen esto en mee taya?_

Where is the changing room?	¿Dónde está el probador?	dondeh estah el probador?
It doesn't fit	No me vale	no me bale
It doesn't suit me	No me queda bien	no me keda byen
Do you have a... size?	¿Tienen una talla...	tyenen oona taya...
- bigger	- mayor?	- mayor?
- smaller	- más pequeña?	- mas pekenya?

Made in Spain

Zara and Mango have brought Spanish fashion to the world, and shoe company Camper is following in their footsteps. Also watch out for the avant-garde shops of Spanish designers in Madrid and Barcelona.

Do you have it/them in...	¿Los/las tienen en...	los/las tyenen en...
- black?	- negro/a?	- negro/a?
- white?	- blanco/a?	- blanko/a?
- blue?	- azul?	- athool?
- green?	- verde?	- berde?
- red?	- rojo/a?	- roho/a?
Are they made of leather?	¿Son de piel?	son de pyel?
I'm going to leave it/them	Lo/s voy a dejar	lo/s boy a dehar
I'll take it/them	Me lo/s quedo	me lo/s kedo

You may hear...

¿Puedo ayudarle?	pwedo ayoodarle?	Can I help you?
¿Le atienden?	le atyenden?	Have you been served?
¿De qué tamaño?	de keh tamanyo?	What size?
No tenemos	no tenemos	We don't have any
Aquí tiene	akee tyene	Here you are

¿Algo más?	*algo mas?*	Anything else?
¿Quiere que se lo envuelva?	*kyero ke se los embwelba?*	Shall I wrap it for you?
Son... (cincuenta) euros	*son... (theenkwenta) eoros*	It's... (50) euros
Está rebajado	*estah rebahado*	It's reduced

Where to shop

Where can I find a...	**¿Dónde hay...**	*dondeh ay...*
- bookshop?	**- una librería?**	*- oona leebrereea?*
- clothes shop?	**- una tienda de ropa?**	*- oona tyenda de ropa?*
- department store?	**- unos grandes almacenes?**	*- oonos grandes almathenes?*
- gift shop?	**- una tienda de regalos?**	*- oona tyenda de regalos?*
- music shop?	**- una tienda de música?**	*- oona tyenda de mooseeka?*
- market?	**- un mercado?**	*- oon merkado?*
- newsagent?	**- un kiosko?**	*- oon keeosko?*
What's the best place to buy...?	**¿Cuál es el mejor sitio para comprar...?**	*kwal es el mehor seeteeo para comprar...?*
I'd like to buy...	**Quisiera comprar...**	*keesyera komprar...*
- a film	**- un carrete de fotos**	*- oon karrete de photos*

Rastro Market

Crowds jam Madrid's flea market on Sunday mornings. Once a slaughterhouse zone, the streets now teem with stalls hawking art, antiques, clothes and all the usual car-boot-sale debris. For lunch, hit one of the area's tapas bars.

- an English newspaper	- **un periódico inglés**	- *oon pereeodeeko eengles*
- a map	- **un mapa**	- *oon mapa*
- postcards	- **postales**	- *postales*

Food markets

Explore a bustling market like Barcelona's La Boquería, a treasure trove of hams, cheeses, wines, preserves and olive oils. Crown a picnic with a confection from Escribà, the sweet shop founded by the "Mozart of Chocolate".

Food & markets

Is there a...nearby?	**¿Hay un...cerca?**	*ay oon...serka?*
- supermarket	- **supermercado**	- *soopermerkado*
- market	- **mercado**	- *merkado*
Can I have...	**¿Me pone...**	*me pone...*
- some bread?	- **pan?**	- *pan?*
- some fruit?	- **fruta?**	- *phroota?*
- some cheese?	- **queso?**	- *keso?*
- a bottle of water?	- **una botella de agua?**	- *oona boteya de agwa?*
- a bottle of wine?	- **una botella de vino?**	- *oona boteya de beeno?*
I'd like... of that	**Quisiera... de eso**	*keesyera... de eso*
- half a kilo	- **medio kilo**	- *medyo keelo*
- 250 grams	- **doscientos cincuenta gramos**	- *dosthyentos theenkwenta gramos*
- a small/big piece	- **un trozo pequeño/grande**	- *oon trotho pekenyo/grande*

Getting around

Getting to Spain is easier than ever. Low-cost airlines now fly to small, regional airports, in addition to the main hubs of Madrid and Barcelona, and established charter gateways such as Málaga and Palma. Reaching your final destination is also a doddle nowadays, with many new motorways and plenty of car hire firms.

But don't overlook public transport, often the most relaxing and inexpensive route. The AVE high-speed train, which zips from Madrid to Seville in 2.5 hours, is a great experience. Look for **tarjetas** (carnets or discount cards), which sometimes stretch across bus, train and metro systems.

Arrival

Given the no-frills-airline boom, visitors are just as likely to arrive in Girona, Bilbao or Murcia as in Madrid or Barcelona. However, these regional airports don't always boast the same service and efficiency as an international hub. Best arrange car hire or transport into town before you leave home.

Where is/are the...	¿Dónde está/están...	_dond_eh esta/estan...
- luggage from flight...?	- el equipaje del vuelo...?	- el ekee_pa_heh del _bwe_lo...?
- luggage trolleys?	- los carros?	- los _ka_rros?
- lost luggage office?	- la oficina de equipaje perdido?	- la ophee_thee_na de ekee_pa_heh per_dee_do?
- buses?	- los autobuses?	- los awto_boo_ses?
- trains?	- los trenes?	- los _tre_nes?
- taxis?	- los taxis?	- los _tak_sees?
- car rental?	- la oficina de alquiler de coches?	- la ophee_thee_na de alkee_ler_ de _ko_ches?
- exit?	- la salida?	- la sa_lee_da
How do I get to hotel ...?	¿Cómo se va al hotel...?	_ko_mo se ba al o_tel_...
My baggage is...	Mi equipaje...	mee ekee_pa_heh...
- lost	- se ha extraviado	- se ah ekstrabee_a_do
- damaged	- está roto	- esta _ro_to
My baggage is stolen	Me han robado mi equipaje	me an ro_ba_do mee ekee_pa_heh

Customs

Visitors from within the EU are usually waved through customs, although sporadic checks occur. A lone official at a sleepy airport could be overwhelmed by the plane-load of tourists arriving. Occasionally queues form, sometimes on the tarmac. Bring a hat, sun block and a water bottle – or winter woollies, as appropriate.

The children are on this passport	Los niños están en este pasaporte	los _neen_yos estan en _es_te pasa_por_teh

We're here on holiday	**Estamos aqui de vacaciones**	*Estamos akee de vakacyones*
I'm going to...	**Voy a...**	*voy a...*
I have nothing to declare	**No tengo nada que declarar**	*no tengo nada ke deklarar*
Do I have to declare this?	**¿Tengo que declarar esto?**	*tengo ke deklarar esto?*

Car hire

Hire cars are available at all international airports and in most resorts. Prices aren't low, so check the fine print: the best deals include unlimited mileage, VAT and **seguro todo riesgo** (full insurance cover). Most companies wait for prebooked customers at the arrivals hall, even for late flights.

Scooters

For Spanish teens, there is only one chic way to get around: on a Vespa (scooter). However, the driver must be over 18 and possess a specific license to ride any real power (bikes over 125cc). Helmets are mandatory for all ages.

I'd like to hire a...	**Me gustaría alquilar...**	*me goostareea alkeelar...*
- car	**- un coche**	*- oon kocheh*
- people carrier	**- un mono-volumen**	*- oon mono boloomen*
with...	**con...**	*kon...*
- air conditioning	**- aire acondicionado**	*- ayreh akondeethyonado*
- automatic transmission	**- transmisión automática**	*- tranmeeseeon awtomateeka*
How much is that for a...	**¿Cuánto cuesta por...**	*kwanto kwesta por...*
- day?	**- un día?**	*- oon deea?*
- week?	**- una semana?**	*- oona semana?*

Does that include...	¿Incluye...	eenklooye...?
- mileage?	- el kilometraje?	- el keelometrahe?
- insurance?	- el seguro?	- el segooro?

On the road

Spain recently enjoyed a road-building boom, fuelled by EU subsidies. Motorways now link most major cities; **autopistas** levy tolls, **autovías** are free. Unsurprisingly, Spaniards drive with more heart than head; yet this always translates into courteousness, not road rage, except in busy city centres.

What is the maximum speed?	¿Cuál es el límite de velocidad?	kwal es el leemeeteh de belotheedad?
Can I park here?	¿Puedo aparcar aquí?	pwedo aparkar akee?
Where is a petrol station?	¿Dónde está la gasolinera?	dondeh esta la gasoleenera?
Please fill up the tank with...	Por favor lléneme el depósito con gasolina...	por fabor yeneme el deposeeto kon gasoleena...
- unleaded	- sin plomo	- seen plomo
- diesel	- diesel	- diesel
- leaded	- super	- sooper

Directions

Is this the road to...?	¿Es esta la carretera a...?	es esta la karretera ah...?
How do I get to...?	¿Cómo se va a...?	komo se ba ah...?
How far is it to...?	¿Qué distancia hay a...?	ke deestanthya ay ah...?
How long will it take to...?	¿Cuánto se tarda a...?	kwanto se tarda ah...?
Could you point it out on the map?	¿Me puede indicar dónde está en el mapa?	me pwedeh eendeekar dondeh esta en el mapa?
I've lost my way	Me he perdido	me eh perdeedo
On the right/left	A la derecha/ izquierda	ah la derecha/eethkyerda
Turn right/left	Gire a la derecha/ izquierda	heere a la derecha/eethkyerda
Straight ahead	Todo recto	todo rekto
Turn around	De la vuelta	deh la bwelta

Public transport

In cities, public transport beats driving hands down. The largest – such as Madrid, Barcelona, Valencia and Bilbao – boast metros; other cities have extensive tram or bus networks. Intercity trains are good, cheap alternatives to hire cars, particularly the high-speed AVE from Madrid to Córdoba and Seville in the South, and Zaragoza and Lleida in the northeast.

Madrid Metro

The capital's metro was opened in 1919 and now has over 200 stations. It will take you almost anywhere in the city and operates from 6am to 1.30am. Buy a Metrobús ticket for 10 journeys.

Bus	**Autobús**	*awto<u>boos</u>*
Bus station	**Estación de autobús**	*estath<u>yon</u> de awto<u>boos</u>*
Train	**Tren**	*tren*
Train station	**Estación de trenes**	*estath<u>yon</u> de <u>trenes</u>*
Ferry	**Ferry**	*<u>fe</u>ree*
Ferry port	**Puerto**	*<u>pwer</u>to*
I'd like to go to...	**Quisiera ir a...**	*kees<u>ye</u>ra eer ah...*
I'd like a... ticket	**Quisiera un billete...**	*kees<u>ye</u>ra oon beey<u>e</u>teh...*
- single	**- de ida**	*- de <u>ee</u>da*
- return	**- de ida y vuelta**	*- de <u>ee</u>da ee <u>bwel</u>ta*
- first class	**- de primera clase**	*- de pri<u>me</u>ra <u>kla</u>se*
- smoking/non-smoking	**- fumador/no-fumador**	*- fooh<u>ma</u>dor/<u>no</u>-fooh<u>ma</u>dor*
What time does it leave/arrive?	**¿A qué hora sale/llega?**	*a ke <u>o</u>ra <u>sah</u>le/<u>ye</u>ga?*
Could you tell me when to get off?	**¿Me puede indicar cuándo me bajo?**	*me <u>pwe</u>de eendee<u>kar</u> <u>kwan</u>do me <u>ba</u>ho?*

Taxis

I'd like a taxi to...	**Quisiera un taxi para ir a...**	*keesyera oon taksee para eer ah...*
How much is it to...	**¿Cuánto cuesta al...**	*kwanto kwesta al...*
- the airport?	**- aeropuerto?**	*- aeropwerto?*
- the town centre?	**- centro?**	*- thentro?*
- hotel...?	**- hotel...?**	*- otel...?*

Tours

Most areas cater to tourists very well, particularly on the Costas and the Islands, and in the big cities. English-speaking guides are usually available, though not in every time slot.

Are there any organised tours of the town/region?	**¿Hay excursiones guiadas de la ciudad/región?**	*ay ekskoorsyones gyadas de la thyoodad/reheeon?*
Where do they leave from?	**¿De dónde salen?**	*de dondeh salen?*
What time does it start?	**¿A qué hora empieza?**	*a ke ora empyetha?*
Do you have English-speaking guides?	**¿Tienen guías que hablan inglés?**	*tyenen gyas ke ablan eengles?*
Is lunch/tea included?	**¿Está incluida la comida/la merienda?**	*esta eenklooyda la komeeda/la meryenda?*
Do we get any free time?	**¿Nos dan algo de tiempo libre?**	*nos dan algo de tyempo leebre?*
Are we going to see...?	**¿Vamos a ver...?**	*bamos a ver...?*
What time do we get back?	**¿A qué hora volvemos?**	*a ke ora bolbemos?*

Accommodation

Travellers have a wide choice of traditional accommodation, such as hotels, apartments and campsites. A more romantic option, however, is bed-and-breakfast in a **finca**, a typical countryside cottage. Also more than 6,000 rural houses are available for rent to those who seek close contact with nature and local customs.

Hostales – not hostels, despite the name – usually rate one to three stars, but **pensiones** range in quality and can even rival posh hotels. **"Residencia"** means the facility lacks a dining room (but may serve breakfast nonetheless).

The country's 90-odd **paradores** remain the most dramatic choice, with locations ranging from medieval castles to former monasteries and hilltop fortresses.

Types of accommodation

Spain has enjoyed an accommodation renaissance of late, adding high-end hotels and refreshing **pensiones** with amenities like Internet access. Those preferring independence and self-catering can rent family villas (possibly with private pools), farmhouses (also good for groups) or village houses.

I'd like to stay in...	**Quisiera alojarme en...**	*keesyera aloharme en...*
- an apartment	**- un apartamento**	*- oon apartamento*
- a campsite	**- un camping**	*- oon kamping*
- a hotel	**- un hotel**	*- oon otel*
- an apart-hotel	**- un apart-hotel**	*- oon apart-otel*
- a youth hostel	**- un albergue juvenil**	*- oon alberge hoobeneel*
- a guest house	**- una pensión**	*- oona pensyon*
Is it...	**¿Es...**	*es...*
- full board?	**- pensión completa?**	*- pensyon kompletta?*
- half board?	**- media pensión?**	*- medya pensyon?*
- self-catering?	**- sin servicio de comidas?**	*- seen serbeethyo de komeedas?*

Live like a king

For a special holiday experience, stay in a **parador**. Although state-owned, these hotels offer real luxury in fabulous buildings and locations. See www.parador.es/english for more information.

Reservations

Do you have any rooms available?	**¿Tienen habitaciones libres?**	*tyenen abeetathyones leebres?*
Can you recommend anywhere else?	**¿Me puede recomendar otro sitio?**	*me pwede rekomendar otro seetyo?*

I'd like to make a reservation for...	**Quiero hacer una reserva para...**	*kyero ather oona reserba para...*
- tonight	**- esta noche**	*- esta noche*
- one night	**- una noche**	*- oona noche*
- two nights	**- dos noches**	*- dos noches*
- a week	**- una semana**	*- oona semana*
From... (May 1st) to... (May 8th)	**Del... (primero de mayo) al... (ocho de mayo)**	*del... (preemero de mayo) al... (ocho de mayo)*

Room types

Hotels usually provide mini bars, TV, telephone and air conditioning. Amenities vary considerably, however, so check before booking. **Parador** hotels have luxurious extras, including a salon area sometimes. On the opposite end, budget travellers should carry a padlock for the door... Regardless of price range, book ahead in peak season. Request a **habitación exterior** (outward-facing room) for air and light; a **habitación interior** for a darker, quieter experience.

Do you have... room?	**¿Tiene una habitación...**	*tyene oona abeetathyon...*
- a single	**- individual?**	*- eendeeveedooal?*
- a double	**- doble?**	*- doble?*
- a family	**- para una familia?**	*- para oona fameelya?*
with...	**con...**	*con...*
- a cot?	**- una cuna?**	*- oona koona?*
- twin beds?	**- dos camas?**	*- dos kamas?*
- a double bed?	**- una cama doble/de matrimonio?**	*- oona kama doble/de matreemonyo?*
- a bath/shower?	**- bañera/ducha?**	*- banyera/doocha?*
- air conditioning?	**- aire acondicionado?**	*- ayre akondeethyonado?*
- internet access?	**- acceso a internet?**	*- aktheso ah eenternet?*
Can I see the room?	**¿Puedo ver la habitación?**	*pwedo ver la abeetathyon?*
How much is...	**¿Cuánto cuesta...**	*kwanto kwesta...*
- a double room?	**- una habitación doble?**	*- oona abeetathyon doble?*

- per night?	**- por noche?**	- por _no_che?
- per week?	**- por semana?**	- por se_ma_na?
Is breakfast included?	**¿Está incluido el desayuno?**	e_stah_ eenkloo_ee_do el desa_yoo_no?
Do you have...	**¿Tienen...**	_ty_enen...
- a reduction for children?	**- descuentos para niños?**	- des_kwen_tos _pa_ra _neen_yos?
- a single room supplement?	**- suplemento por habitación individual?**	- soople_men_to _pa_ra abeeta_thyon_ een-deeveedoo_al_?

Prices

Unsurprisingly, rates increase with the number of stars – though the quality may not. VAT is sometimes included; breakfast usually requires a supplement (or just fuel up at a nearby café like the locals). **Paradors** are rather expensive and should be reserved well in advance. Tipping is not obligatory, but it is the norm, except in less touristy northern areas.

Is there...	**¿Hay...**	ay...
- a swimming pool?	**- piscina?**	- pees_thee_na?
- an elevator?	**- ascensor?**	- asthen_sor_?
I'll take it	**La cojo**	la _ko_ho
Can I pay by...	**¿Puedo pagar con...**	_pwe_do pa_gar_ kon...
- credit card?	**- tarjeta de crédito?**	- tar_het_ta de _kre_dee-to?
- travellers' cheque?	**- cheques de viaje?**	- _che_kes de bee_a_-he?

Finca tip

Fincas (countryside cottages), farmhouses and family villas are a welcome respite from the tourist hotspots. Explore off the beaten track, discovering local colour and character.

Hotels with handicaps
A lot of greens have appeared among the landscape's browns in recent years. Golf hotels, now spread all over the country, offer courses, pro shops and – quite often – luxurious amenities.

Special requests

Could you...	¿Podría...	podreea...
- put this in the hotel safe?	- poner esto en la caja de seguridad del hotel?	- poner esto en la kaha de segooreedath del otel?
- order a taxi for me?	- pedirme un taxi?	- pedeerme oon taksee?
- wake me up at (7am)?	- despertarme a las (siete) de la mañana?	- despertarme a las (syete) de la manyana?
Can I have...	¿Quiero una habitación...	kyero oona abeetathyon...
- a room with a sea view?	- con vista al mar?	- kon beesta al mar?
- a bigger room?	- más grande?	- mas grande?
- a quieter room?	- más tranquila?	- mas trankeela?
Is there...	¿Hay...	ay...
- a safe?	- caja de seguridad?	- kaha de segooreedath?
- a babysitting service?	- servicio de canguro?	- serbeethyo kan-gooro?
- a laundry service?	- servicio de lavandería?	- serbeethyo de labandereea?
Is there wheelchair access?	¿Hay acceso para silla de ruedas?	ay aktheso para seeya de rwedas?

Checking in & out

I have a reservation for tonight	**Tengo una reserva para esta noche**	_tengo oona reserba para esta noche_
In the name of...	**A nombre de...**	_a nombre de..._
Here's my passport	**Aquí tiene mi pasaporte**	_akee tyene mee pasaporte_
What time is check out?	**¿A qué hora hay que dejar la habitación?**	_a keh ora ay ke dehar la abeetathyon?_
Can I have a later check out?	**¿Puedo salir más tarde?**	_pwedo saleer mas tarde?_
Can I leave my bags here?	**¿Puedo dejar mis maletas aquí?**	_pwedo dehar mees maletas akee?_
I'd like to check out	**Quiero marcharme**	_kyero marcharme_
Can I have the bill?	**¿Me da la cuenta?**	_me da la kwenta?_

Camping

Do you have...	**¿Tienen...**	_tyenen..._
- a site available?	**- un espacio libre?**	- _un espathyo leebre?_
- electricity?	**- electricidad?**	- _elektreetheedath?_
- hot showers?	**- duchas con agua caliente?**	- _doochas kon agwa kalyente?_
- tents for hire?	**- tiendas para alquilar?**	- _tyendas para alkeelar?_
How much is it per...	**¿Cuánto cuesta por...**	_kwanto kwesta por.._
- tent?	**- tienda?**	- _tyenda?_
- caravan?	**- caravana?**	- _karabana?_
- person?	**- persona?**	- _persona?_
- car?	**- coche?**	- _koche?_
Where is/are the...	**¿Dónde está/están...**	_dondeh estah/estan..._
- reception?	**- la recepción?**	- _la rethepthyon?_
- bathrooms?	**- los baños?**	- _los banyos?_
- washing facilities?	**- la lavandería?**	- _la labandereea?_

Survival guide

In most Spanish cities, banks open from 9am to 2pm on weekdays and some on Saturday mornings too. Withdraw euros from ATMs with a UK debit or credit card (it's wise to register your itinerary beforehand, when travelling abroad). Banks typically provide a better rate than Bureaux de Change.

Internet cafés abound, except in quite remote areas. Spaniards love children, so attractions for little ones are ample. Travellers with disabilities, however, will often feel uncatered for, although this will be compensated more often than not by people's helpfulness.

Money & banks

Where is the nearest...	¿Dónde está... más cercano?	*dondeh esta... mas therkano?*
- bank?	- el banco	*- el banko*
- ATM/bank machine?	- el cajero automático	*- el kahero owtomateeko*
Where is the nearest foreign exchange office?	¿Dónde está la oficina para cambiar dinero más cercana?	*dondeh esta la ofeetheena para kambyar deenero mas therkana?*
I'd like to...	Quisiera...	*keesyera...*
- withdraw money	- sacar dinero	*- sakar deenero*
- cash a traveller's cheque	- cobrar un cheque de viaje	*- kobrar oon chekeh de beeaheh*
- change money	- cambiar dinero	*- kambyar deenero*
- arrange a transfer	- hacer una transferencia	*- ather oona transferenthya*
Could I have smaller notes, please?	¿Me da billetes más pequeños por favor?	*me dah beeyetes mas pekenyos por fabor?*

Bank on formality

The atmosphere in most banks can be quite formal. Not surprisingly, staff members are well regarded and have a very high status in Spanish society.

What's the exchange rate?	¿A cuánto está el cambio?	*a kwanto esta el kambyo?*
What's the commission?	¿Cuánto es la comisión?	*kwanto es la komeesyon?*
What's the charge for...	¿Cuánto es la comisión por...	*kwanto es la komeesyon por...*

- making a withdrawal?	**- sacar dinero?**	*- sakar deenero*
- exchanging money?	**- cambiar dinero?**	*- kambyar deenero*
- cashing a cheque?	**- cobrar un cheque?**	*- kobrar oon chekeh*
What's the minimum/ maximum amount?	**¿Cuál es la cantidad mínima/máxima?**	*kwal es la kanteedad meeneema/makseema?*
This is not right	**Esto no es correcto**	*esto no es korrekto*
Is there a problem with my account?	**¿Hay algún problema con mi cuenta?**	*ai algoon problema kon mee kwenta?*
The ATM/bank machine took my card	**El cajero se ha tragado mi tarjeta**	*el kahero se a tragado mee tarhetta*
I've forgotten my PIN	**Se me ha olvidado el PIN**	*se me a olbeedado el peen*

Post office

Where is the (main) post office?	**¿Dónde está la oficina (central) de correos?**	*dondeh esta la opheetheena thentral de korreos?*
I'd like to send a...	**Quisiera enviar...**	*keesyera enbyar...*
- letter	**- una carta**	*- oona karta*
- postcard	**- una postal**	*- oona postal*
- parcel	**- un paquete**	*- oon paketeh*
- fax	**- un fax**	*- oon phax*
I'd like to send this...	**Quisiera enviar esto...**	*keesyera enbyar esto*
- to the United Kingdom	**- al Reino Unido**	*- al reyno ooneedo*
- by airmail	**- por avión**	*- por abyon*
- by express mail	**- por correo urgente**	*- por korreo oorhenteh*
- by registered mail	**- por correo certificado**	*- por korreo thairteefeekado*
I'd like...	**Quisiera...**	*keesyera...*
- a stamp for this letter/postcard	**- un sello para esta carta/postal**	*- oon seyo para esta karta/postal*

51

- to buy envelopes	**- comprar sobres**	*- komprar sobres*
- to make a photocopy	**- hacer una fotocopia**	*- ather oona photokopya*
It's fragile	**Es frágil**	*es phraheel*

Postcards and parcels

The Spanish postal service has improved in recent years and it's unusual to hear of lost items. Service is fast and reliable, and you won't miss the ubiquitous bright yellow post boxes.

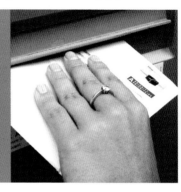

Telecoms

Where can I make an international phone call?	**¿Dónde puedo hacer una llamada internacional?**	*dondeh pwedo ather oona yamada eenternathyonal?*
Where can I buy a phone card?	**¿Dónde puedo comprar una tarjeta de teléfono?**	*dondeh pwedo komprar oona tarhetta de telephono?*
How do I call abroad?	**¿Cómo llamo al extranjero?**	*komo yamo al ekstranhero?*
How much does it cost per minute?	**¿Cuánto cuesta por minuto?**	*kwanto kwesta por meenooto?*
The number is...	**El número es...**	*el noomero es...*
What's the area/country code for...?	**¿Cuál es el prefijo de la región/del país...?**	*kwal es el prepheeho de la rehyon/de pays...?*
The number is engaged	**Está comunicando**	*esta komooneekando*
The connection is bad	**No se oye bien**	*no se oye byen*
I've been cut off	**Se ha cortado**	*se a kortado*

I'd like...	**Quisiera...**	*keesyera...*
- a charger for my mobile phone	**- un cargador para el móvil**	*- oon kargador para el mobeel*
- an adaptor plug	**- un adaptador**	*- oon adaptador*
- a pre-paid SIM card	**- una tarjeta prepago**	*- oona tarhetta prepag*

Internet

Is there an Internet café near here?	**¿Hay un internet café cerca de aquí?**	*ai oon eenternet kafe therka de akee?*
Can I access the Internet here?	**¿Tienen acceso a internet?**	*tyenen aktheso a eenternet?*
I'd like to...	**Quisiera...**	*keesyera...*
- use the Internet	**- usar Internet**	*- oosar eenternet*
- check my email	**- leer mis emails**	*- ler mees eemeyls*
- use a printer	**- usar la impresora**	*- oosar la eempresora*
How much is it...	**¿Cuánto cuesta...**	*kwanto kwesta...*
- per minute?	**- por minuto?**	*- por meenooto?*
- per hour?	**- por hora?**	*- por ora?*
- to buy a CD?	**- comprar un CD?**	*- komprar oon thedeh?*
How do I...	**¿Cómo...**	*komo..?*
- log on?	**- entro al sistema?**	*- entro al seestema?*
- open a browser?	**- abro el navegador?**	*- abro el nabegador?*
- print this?	**- imprimo esto?**	*- eempreemo esto?*
I need help with this computer	**Necesito ayuda con este ordenador**	*netheseeto ayooda kon este ordenador*
The computer has crashed	**Se ha colgado el ordenador**	*se a kolgado el ordenador*
I've finished	**He terminado**	*e termeenado*

Chemist

Where's the nearest (all-night) pharmacy?	**¿Hay una farmacia (de guardia) cerca?**	*ai oona pharmathya (de gwardeea) therka?*

At what time does the pharmacy open/close?	¿A qué hora abre/cierra la farmacia?	a keh ora abre/thyerra la pharmathya?
I need something for...	Necesito algo para...	netheseeto algo para...
- diarrhoea	- la diarrea	- la dyarea
- a cold	- el resfriado	- el resphryado
- a cough	- la tos	- la tos
- insect bites	- las picaduras de insecto	- las peekadooras de eensekto
- sunburn	- las quemaduras de sol	- las kemadooras de sol
- motion sickness	- el mareo	- el mareo
- hay fever	- la alergia al polen	- la alerhya al polen
- period pain	- el dolor de regla	- el dolor de regla
- abdominal pains	- el dolor abdominal	- el dolor abdomeenal
- a urine infection	- la infección urinaria	- la eenphekthyon ooreenaria
- a vaginal infection	- la infección vaginal	- la eenphekthyon vaheenal
I'd like...	Quisiera...	keesyera...
- aspirin	- aspirinas	- apeereenas
- plasters	- tiritas	- teereetas
- condoms	- condones	- kondones
- insect repellent	- crema anti-insectos	- krema antee-eensektos
- painkillers	- calmantes	- kalmantes
- a contraceptive	- un anticonceptivo	- un antikontheptibo
How much should I take?	¿Cuánto tomo?	kwanto tomo?
Take...	Tome...	tome...
- a tablet	- una pastilla	- oona pasteeya
- a teaspoon	- una cucharada	- oona koocharada
- with water	- con agua	- kon agwa
How often should I take this?	¿Cuántas veces lo tomo?	kwantas bethes lo tomo?

- once/twice a day	- una vez/dos veces al día	- *oona beth/dos bethes al deea*
- before/after meals	- antes/después de las comidas	- *antes/despwes de las komeedas?*
- in the morning/evening	- por la mañana/por la noche	- *por la manyana/por la noche*
Is it suitable for children?	¿Lo pueden tomar los niños?	*lo pweden tomar los neenyos?*
Will it make me drowsy?	¿Me va a dar sueño?	*me ba a dar swenyo?*
Do I need a prescription?	¿Es con receta?	*es kon retheta?*
I have a prescription	Tengo una receta	*tengo oona retheta*

Ask your chemist
Spanish pharmacists are well trained and generally willing to give advice on any ailments. Many medicines are dispensed **sin receta** (over the counter), so don't be afraid to ask!

Children
Where should I take the children?	¿Dónde llevo a los niños?	*dondeh yebo a los neenyos?*
Where is the nearest...	¿Hay...cerca?	*ai...therka?*
- playground?	- una zona de juegos	- *oona thona de hwegos*
- fairground?	- un parque de atracciones	- *oon parkeh de atrakthyones*
- zoo?	- un zoo	- *oon thoh*
- swimming pool?	- una piscina	- *oona peestheena*
- park?	- un parque	- *oon parkeh*
Is this suitable for children?	¿Es apropiado para niños?	*es apropyado para neenyos?*

Are children allowed?	¿Pueden entrar niños?	*pweden entrar neenyos?*
Are there baby-changing facilities here?	¿Hay cambiadores para bebés aquí?	*ai kambyadores para bebes akee?*
Do you have...	¿Tienen...	*tyenen...*
- a children's menu?	- menú infantil?	*- menoo eenphanteel?*
- a high chair?	- tronas para bebés?	*- tronas para bebes?*
Is there...	¿Hay...	*ai..*
- a child-minding service?	- canguros?	*- kangooros?*
- a nursery?	- guardería?	*- gwarderya?*
Can you recommend a reliable babysitter?	¿Me puede recomendar una canguro de confianza?	*me pwede rekomendar oona kangooro de konpheeantha?*
Are the children constantly supervised?	¿Vigilan a los niños continuamente?	*beeheelan ah los neenyos konteenwamente?*
When can I bring them?	¿Cuándo puedo traerlos?	*kwando pwedo trayerlos?*
What time do I have to pick them up?	¿A qué hora los recojo?	*ah ke ora los rekoho?*
He/she is ... years old	El/ella tiene... años	*El/eya tyeneh... anyos*
I'd like to buy...	Quisiera comprar...	*keesyera komprar...*
- nappies	- pañales	*- panyales*
- baby wipes	- toallitas húmedas para bebés	*- toayeetas oomedas para bebes*
- tissues	- pañuelos	*- panwelos*

Travellers with disabilities

I have a disability	Soy discapacitado	*soy deeskapatheetado*
I need assistance	Necesito ayuda	*netheseeto ayooda*
I am blind	Soy ciego	*soy thyego*

I am deaf	**Soy sordo**	*soy sordo*
I have a hearing aid	**Llevo un aparato para sordos**	*yebo oon aparato para sordos*
I can't walk well	**No ando bien**	*no ando byen*
Is there a lift?	**¿Hay ascensor?**	*ai asthensor?*
Is there wheelchair access?	**¿Hay acceso para sillas de ruedas?**	*ai aktheso para seeyas de rwedas?*
Can I bring my guide dog?	**¿Puedo traer a mi perro guía?**	*pwedo traer ah mee perro gya?*
Are there disabled toilets?	**¿Hay baños para discapacitados?**	*ai banyos para deeskapatheeta-dos?*
Do you offer disabled services?	**¿Tienen servicios para discapacitados?**	*tyenen serbeethyos para deeskapathee-tados?*
Could you help me...	**¿Me puede ayudar a...**	*me pwede ayoodar ah...*
- cross the street?	**- cruzar la calle?**	*- kroothar la kaye?*
- go up/down the stairs?	**- subir/bajar las escaleras?**	*- soobeer/bahar las eskaleras?*
Can I sit down somewhere?	**¿Me puedo sentar en algún sitio?**	*me pwedo sentar en algoon seetyo?*
Could you call a disabled taxi for me?	**¿Puede llamar un taxi para discapacitados?**	*pwede yamar oon taksee para deeskapatheeta-dos?*

Repairs & cleaning

This is broken	**Esto está roto**	*esto estah roto*
Can you fix it?	**¿Puede arreglarlo?**	*pwede arreglarlo?*
Do you have...	**¿Tiene...**	*tyene...*
- a battery?	**- una batería?**	*- oona batereea?*
- spare parts?	**- piezas de recambio?**	*- pyethas de rekambyo?*
Can you...this?	**¿Puede...esto?**	*pwede...esto?*
- clean	**- limpiar**	*- leempyar*
- press	**- planchar**	*- planchar*
- dry-clean	**- lavar en seco**	*- Lavar en seko*
- patch	**- arreglar**	*- arreglar*

| When will it be ready? | ¿Cuándo estará listo? | *kwando estarah leesto?* |
| This isn't mine | Esto no es mío | *esto no es meeo* |

Tourist information

Where's the Tourist Information Office?	¿Dónde está la oficina de turismo?	*dondeh esta la opheetheena de tooreesmo?*
Do you have a city/regional map?	¿Tiene un plano de la ciudad/región?	*tyene oon plano de la thyoodad/rehyon?*
What are the main places of interest?	¿Cuáles son los principales lugares de interés?	*kwales son los preentheepales loogares de eenteres?*
Could you show me on the map?	¿Me puede indicar dónde está en el plano?	*me pwede eendeekar dondeh estah en el plano?*
We'll be here for...	Estaremos aquí por...	*estaremos akee por...*
- half a day	- medio día	*- medyo deea*
- a day	- un día	*- oon deea*
- a week	- una semana	*- oona semana*
Do you have a brochure in English?	¿Tiene un folleto en inglés?	*tyene oon phoyeto en eengles?*
We're interested in...	Nos interesa...	*nos eenteresa...*
- history	- la historia	*- lah eestorya*
- architecture	- la arquitectura	*- lah arkeetektoora*
- shopping	- ir de compras	*- eer de kompras*
- a scenic walk	- un paseo	*- oon paseo*
- a guided tour	- una visita guiada	*- oona beeseeta gyada*
What days is it open/closed?	¿Qué días abre/cierra?	*ke deeas abre/thyera?*
What time does it open/close?	¿A qué hora abre/cierra?	*a ke ora abre/thyera?*
What's the admission price?	¿Cuánto cuesta la entrada?	*kwanto kwesta la entrada?*
Are there any tours in English?	¿Hay alguna visita en inglés?	*ai algoona beeseeta en eengles?*

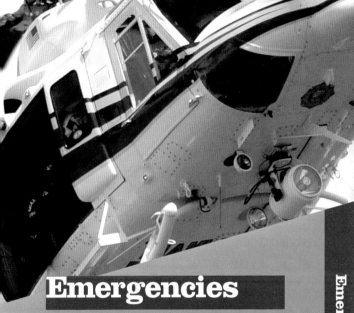

Emergencies

Although no more dangerous than other Western European countries, Spain's crime rate is rising, especially in major cities such as Madrid, Barcelona and Seville. Street robberies and thefts are the most common misdemeanours, so keep an eye on your belongings. Also be alert in resort areas, where pickpocketing, burglary and vehicle break-ins occur more frequently nowadays.

EU residents, including Brits, are entitled to free medical care. However, the European Health Insurance Card (EHIC) only covers emergency treatment and private hospitals won't accept it. For this reason it is recommended you buy travel insurance before travelling to Spain.

Medical

Where is...	¿Dónde está...	dondeh estah...
- the hospital?	- el hospital?	- el ospeetal?
- the health centre?	- el ambulatorio?	- el amboolatoryo?
I need...	Necesito...	netheseeto...
- a doctor	- un médico	- oon medeeko
- a female doctor	- una doctora	- oona doktora
- an ambulance	- una ambulancia	- oona amboolanthya
It's very urgent	Es muy urgente	es muy oorhente
I'm injured	Estoy herido/a	estoy ereedo/a
Can I see the doctor?	¿Puedo ver al médico?	pwedo ver al medeeko?
I don't feel well	No me siento bien	no me syento byen
I have...	Tengo...	tengo...
- a cold	- un resfriado	- un resphryado
- diarrhoea	- diarrea	- deearrea
- a rash	- un sarpullido	- oon sarpooyeedo
- a temperature	- fiebre	- phyebre
I have a lump here	Tengo un bulto aquí	tengo oon boolto akee
Can I have the morning-after pill?	¿Me da la píldora del día después?	me da la peeldora despwes?
It hurts here	Me duele aquí	me dwele akee
It hurts a lot/a little	Me duele mucho/poco	me dwele moocho/poko
How much do I owe you?	¿Cuánto le debo?	kwanto le debo?
I have insurance	Tengo seguro	tengo segooro

Dentist

I need a dentist	Necesito ver a un dentista	netheseeto ver a oon denteesta
I have tooth ache	Tengo dolor de muelas	tengo dolor de mooelas
My gums are swollen	Tengo las encías inflamadas	tengo las entheeas eenphlamadas
This filling has fallen out	Se me ha caído este empaste	se me a kaeedo este empaste
I have an abscess	Tengo un flemón	tengo oon phlemon

I've broken a tooth	**Me he roto un diente**	*me e rotto oon dyente*
Are you going to take it out?	**¿Me va a sacar la muela?**	*me ba a sakar la mooela?*
Can you fix it temporarily?	**¿Lo puede arreglar provisional-mente?**	*lo pwede arreglar probeesyonal-mente?*

Crime

I want to report a theft	**Quiero denunciar un robo**	*kyero denoonthyar oon robo*
Someone has stolen my...	**Me han robado...**	*me an robado*
- bag	**- la bolsa**	*- la bolsa*
- car	**- el coche**	*- el koche*
- credit cards	**- las tarjetas de crédito**	*- las tarhettas de kredeeto*
- money	**- el dinero**	*- el deenero*
- passport	**- el pasaporte**	*- el pasaporte*
I've been attacked	**Me han agredido**	*me an agredeedo*

Accident report

For any accident, however minor, you must make a **denuncia** (a report) to the Spanish police. You can do this at the nearest police station, but also by phone or even Internet.

Lost property

I've lost my...	**He perdido...**	*e perdeedo...*
- car keys	**- las llaves del coche**	*- las yabes del koche*
- driving licence	**- el carnet de conducir**	*- el karneh de kon-dootheer*
- handbag	**- el bolso**	*- el bolso*
- flight tickets	**- los billetes de avión**	*- los beeyetes de abyon*

It happened...	Ocurrió...	okoorryo...
- this morning	- esta mañana	- esta manyana
- today	- hoy	- oy
- in the hotel	- en el hotel	- en el otel
I left it in the taxi	Lo/a dejé en el taxi	lo/a deheh en el taksee

Breakdowns

I've had...	He tenido...	he teneedo...
- an accident	- un accidente	- oon akseedente
- a breakdown	- una avería	- oona abereea
- a puncture	- un pinchazo	- oon peenchatho

My battery is flat	No tengo batería	no tengo batereea
I don't have a spare tyre	No tengo rueda de repuesto	no tengo rooeda de repwesto
I've run out of petrol	Me he quedado sin gasolina	me e kedado seen gasoleena
My car doesn't start	No me arranca el coche	no me arranka el koche

Can you repair it?	¿Puede arreglarlo?	pwede arreglarlo?
How long will you be?	¿Cuánto va a tardar?	kwanto ba a tardar?
I have breakdown cover	Tengo seguro de asistencia en carretera	tengo segooro de aseestenthya en karretera

Problems with the authorities

I'm sorry, I didn't realise...	Lo siento, no me dí cuenta de que...	lo syento, no me dee kwenta de ke...
- I was driving so fast	- conducía tan rápido	- kondootheea tan rapeedo
- I went over the red lights	- me salté el semáforo en rojo	- me salteh el semaphoro en roho
- it was against the law	- eso era ilegal	- eso era eelegal

Here are my documents	Aquí tiene mis documentos	akee tyene mees dokoomentos
I'm innocent	Soy inocente	soy eenothente

No me parece que esto ... una utopía.
B. era
estaría

Roberto, estoy sin un cobre. Tengo
¿A quién ... venderás?
B. te lo
A. se

Disculpa Marcos, la solución qu
B. a el/correc
A. al/adecuada

¿Me puedes explicar por qué
B. dices
A. niegas

Dictionary

This section consists of two parts: an
English-Spanish dictionary to help
you get your point across and a
Spanish-English one to decipher the
reply. In the Spanish, we list nouns
with their article: **el** for masculine, **la**
for feminine and **los** or **las** for plural.
If nouns can be either masculine or
feminine, we display both: **el/la niño/a**
(child) means **el niño** is a male child
(i.e. a boy), **la niña** the female version
(a girl). For adjectives we do the same:
"-o" is the masculine form (**niño
cansado** – tired boy), "-a" the feminine
(**niña cansada** – tired girl).

English-Spanish dictionary

A

a(n)	**un/a**	*oon/a*
about (concerning)	**sobre**	*sobre*
accident	**el accidente**	*el aktheedente*
accommodation	**el alojamiento**	*el alohamyento*
A&E	**urgencias**	*oorhentheeas*
aeroplane	**el avión**	*el abyon*
again	**otra vez**	*otra beth*
ago	**hace**	*athe*
AIDS	**el SIDA**	*el seeda*
airmail	**el correo aéreo**	*el korreo aereo*
airport	**el aeropuerto**	*el aeropooerto*
alarm	**la alarma**	*la alarma*
all	**todo/a(s)**	*todo/a(s)*
all right	**de acuerdo**	*de akwerdo*
allergy	**la alergia**	*la alerhya*
ambulance	**la ambulancia**	*la amboolanthya*
America	**América**	*amereeka*
American	**americano/a**	*amereekano/a*
and	**y**	*ee*

anniversary	**el aniversario**	*el aneebersaryo*

Celebrating anniversaries is a national pastime in Spain: seven bank holidays mark such events, from Columbus's birthday to the overthrow of Franco.

another	**otro/a(s)**	*otro/a(s)*
to answer	**responder**	*responder*
any	**alguno/a(s) / ninguno/a(s)**	*algoono/a(s) ningoono/a(s)*
apartment	**el apartamento**	*el apartamento*
appointment	**la cita**	*la theeta*
April	**abril**	*abreel*
area	**el área**	*el areya*
area code	**el prefijo**	*el prepheeho*
around	**alrededor (de)**	*alrededor (de)*
to arrange	**organizar**	*organeethar*
arrival	**la llegada**	*la yegada*
art	**el arte**	*el arte*
to ask	**preguntar**	*pregoontar*
aspirin	**la aspirina**	*la aspeereena*
at	**en**	*en*
August	**agosto**	*agosto*
Australia	**Australia**	*awstralya*
Australian	**australiano/a**	*awstralyano/a*
available	**disponible**	*deesponeeble*
away	**lejos**	*lehos*

B

baby	**el bebé**	*el bebeh*
back (place)	**atrás**	*atras*
baggage	**el equipaje**	*el ekeepahe*

| bar (pub) | **el bar** | *el bar* |
| bath | **el baño** | *el banyo* |

bathing cap   **el gorro de baño**   *el gorro de banyo*
In most public swimming pools, bathing caps are compulsory. Hotel pools are often more forgiving.

to be	**ser / estar**	*ser / estar*
beach	**la playa**	*la playa*
because	**porque**	*porkeh*
best	**el/la/lo mejor**	*el/la/lo mehor*
better	**mejor**	*mehor*
between	**entre**	*entre*
bicycle	**la bicicleta**	*la beetheekletta*
big	**grande**	*grande*
bill	**la cuenta**	*la kwenta*
bit (a)	**un poco**	*un poko*
boarding card	**la tarjeta de embarque**	*la tarhetta de embarkeh*
book	**el libro**	*el leebro*
to book	**reservar**	*reserbar*
booking	**la reserva**	*la reserba*
box office	**la taquilla**	*la takeeya*
boy	**el chico**	*el cheeko*
brother	**el hermano**	*el ermano*
bullfight	**la corrida de toros**	*la korreeda de torros*
bureau de change	**la oficina de cambio**	*la opheetheena de kambyo*
to burn	**quemar**	*kemar*
bus	**el autobús**	*el awtoboos*
business	**el negocio**	*el negothyo*
business class	**la clase preferente**	*la klase prepherente*
but	**pero**	*pero*
to buy	**comprar**	*komprar*
by (via)	**por**	*por*
by (beside)	**al lado (de)**	*al lado (de)*
by (by air, car, etc)	**en avión, en coche, etc**	*en abyon, en koche*

C

café	**la cafetería**	*la kaphetereea*
calculator	**la calculadora**	*la kalkooladora*
to call	**llamar**	*yamar*
camera	**la cámara fotográfica**	*la kamara photographeeka*
can (to be able)	**poder**	*poder*
to cancel	**cancelar**	*kanthelar*
car	**el coche**	*el koche*
carton (cigarettes)	**el cartón**	*el karton*
cash	**el dinero en efectivo**	*el deenero en ephekteebo*
cash point	**el cajero automático**	*el kahero awtomateeko*
casino	**el casino**	*el kaseeno*

cathedral   **la catedral**   *la katedral*
The cathedral of Seville is Spain's largest and ranks third in Europe.

CD	el cd	el thedeh
centre	el centro	el thentro
to change	cambiar	kambyar
charge	el precio	el prethyo
to charge	cobrar	kobrar
cheap	barato/a	barato/a
to check in (airport)	facturar	phaktoorar
to check in (hotel)	registrarse	reheestrarse
cheque	el cheque	el chekeh
child	el/la niño/a	el/la neenyo/a
cigar	el puro	el puro
cigarette	el cigarrillo	el theegareeyo
cinema	el cine	el theene
city	la ciudad	la theeoodath
to close	cerrar	therrar
close by	cerca de	therka de
closed	cerrado/a	therrado/a
clothes	la ropa	la ropa
club	el club	el kloob
coast	la costa	la kosta
cold	frío/a	phreeo/a
colour	el color	el kolor
to complain	reclamar	reklamar
complaint	la reclamación	la reklamathyon
to confirm	confirmar	konpheermar
confirmation	la confirmación	la konpheermathyon
congratulations!	¡enhorabuena!	enorabwena!
consulate	el consulado	el konsoolado
to contact	ponerse en contacto	ponerse en kontakto
contagious	contagioso/a	kontahyoso/a
cool	fresco/a	phresko/a
cost	el precio	el prethyo
to cost	costar	kostar
cot	la cuna	la koona
country	el país	el pays
countryside	el campo	el kampo
cream	la crema	la krema
credit card	la tarjeta de crédito	la tarhetta de kredeeto
crime	el delito	el deleeto

| **currency** | **la moneda** | *la moneda* |

In 2002, Spain replaced the **peseta** with the euro, the
single currency of 12 EU member states now.

customer	el cliente	el klyente
customs	la aduana	la adooana
cut	el corte	el korte
to cut	cortar	kortar
cycling	el ciclismo	el theekleesmo

D

damage	el/los daño/s	el/los danyo/s
date (calendar)	la fecha	la phecha
daughter	la hija	la eeha
day	el día	el deea

December	diciembre	*deethyembre*
to dehydrate	desidratar	*deseedratar*
delay	el retraso	*el retraso*
to dial	marcar	*markar*
difficult	difícil	*deepheethyl*
dining room	el comedor	*el komedor*
directions	las instrucciones	*las eenstrookthyones*
dirty	sucio/a	*soothyo/a*
disable	discapacitado/a	*deeskapatheetado/a*
disco	la discoteca	*la deeskoteka*
discount	el descuento	*el deskwento*
disinfectant	el desinfectante	*el deseenphektante*
to disturb	molestar	*molestar*
doctor	el/la médico/a	*el/la medeeko/a*
double	doble	*doble*
down	abajo	*abaho*
to drive	conducir	*kondootheer*
driver	el/la conductor/a	*el/la kondooktor/a*
driving licence	el permiso de conducir	*el permeeso de kondootheer*
drug	la medicina	*la medeetheena*
to dry clean	lavar en seco	*labar en sekko*
dry cleaners'	la tintorería	*la teentorereea*
during	durante	*doorante*
duty (tax)	los impuestos	*los eempooestos*

E

early	temprano	*temprano*
to eat	comer	*komer*
e-mail	el correo electrónico	*el korreo elektroneeko*
embassy	la embajada	*la embahada*
emergency	la emergencia	*la emerhenthya*
England	Inglaterra	*eenglaterra*

| **English** | **inglés/esa** | *eengles/esa* |

The English love Spain: thousands move southwards every year in search of a new life in the sun.

to enjoy	divertirse	*deeberteerse*
enough	bastante	*bastante*
error	el error	*el error*
exactly	exactamente	*eksaktamente*
exchange rate	el cambio	*el kambeeo*
exhibition	la exposición	*la eksposeethyon*
to export	exportar	*eksportar*
express (delivery)	urgente	*oorhente*
express (train)	rápido	*rapeedo*

F

facilities	las instalaciones	*las eenstalathyones*
far	lejos	*lehos*
fast	rápido/a	*rapeedo/a*
father	el padre	*el padre*
favourite	favorito/a	*faboreeto/a*
to fax	mandar por fax	*mandar por phaks*

English	Spanish	Pronunciation
February	**febrero**	*febrero*
filling (station)	**la gasolinera**	*la gasoleenera*
film (camera)	**el carrete**	*el karrete*
film (cinema)	**la película**	*la peleecoola*
to finish	**terminar**	*termeenar*
fire	**el fuego**	*el phooego*
first aid	**los primeros auxilios**	*los preemeros awkseelyos*
fitting room	**el probador**	*el probador*
flight	**el vuelo**	*el booelo*
flu	**la gripe**	*la greepe*
food poisoning	**la intoxicación alimenticia**	*la eentokseekathyon aleementeethya*
football	**el fútbol**	*el phootbol*
for	**por / para**	*por/para*
form (document)	**el impreso**	*el eempreso*
free (vacant)	**libre**	*leebre*
free (money)	**gratis**	*gratees*
friend	**amigo/a**	*ameego/a*
from	**de / desde**	*de / desde*

G

gallery	**la galería**	*la galereea*
garage	**el garage**	*el garahe*
gas	**el gas**	*el gas*
gents	**los servicios de caballeros**	*los serbeethyos de kabayeros*
to get	**obtener**	*obtener*
girl	**la chica**	*la cheeka*
to give	**dar**	*dar*
glasses	**las gafas**	*las gaphas*
to go	**ir**	*eer*
golf	**el golf**	*el golph*

golf course	**el campo de golf**	*el kampo de golf*

More than 250 golf courses are spread throughout the country and another 150 are planned.

good	**bueno/a**	*bweno/a*
group	**el grupo**	*el groopo*
guarantee	**la garantía**	*la garanteea*
guide	**la guía**	*la geea*

H

hair	**el pelo**	*el pelo*
hairdressers'	**la peluquería**	*la pelookereea*
half	**medio/a**	*medeeo/a*
to have	**tener**	*tener*
heat	**el calor**	*el kalor*
help!	**¡socorro!**	*sokorro!*
to help	**ayudar**	*ayoodar*
here	**aquí**	*akee*
high	**alto/a**	*alto/a*
to hire	**alquilar**	*alkeelar*
holiday	**la fiesta**	*la fyesta*

holidays	**las vacaciones**	*las bakathyones*
homosexual	**homosexual**	*omoseksooal*
horse riding	**montar a caballo**	*montar ah kabayo*
hospital	**el hospital**	*el ospeetal*
hot	**caliente**	*kalyente*
how?	**¿cómo?**	*komo?*
how big?	**¿de qué tamaño?**	*de ke tamanyo?*
how far?	**¿a qué distancia?**	*a ke deestanthya*
how long?	**¿cuánto tiempo?**	*kwanto tyempo?*
how much?	**¿cuánto?**	*kwanto?*
to be hungry	**tener hambre**	*tener ambre*
hurry up!	**¡de prisa!**	*de preesa!*
to hurt	**doler**	*doler*
husband	**el marido**	*el mareedo*

I

identity card	**el carnet de identidad**	*el karneh de eedenteedath*
ill	**enfermo/a**	*enfermo/a*
immediately	**inmediatamente**	*eenmedyatamente*
to import	**importar**	*eemportar*
important	**importante**	*eemportante*
in	**en**	*en*
information	**la información**	*la eenphormathyon*
inside	**dentro (de)**	*dentro (de)*
insurance	**el seguro**	*el segooro*
interesting	**interesante**	*eenteresante*
international	**internacional**	*eenternathyonal*
Ireland	**Irlanda**	*eerlanda*
Irish	**irlandés/esa**	*eerlandes/esa*
island	**la isla**	*la eesla*
itinerary	**el itinerario**	*el eeteeneraryo*

J

January	**enero**	*enero*
jellyfish	**la medusa**	*la medoosa*
jet ski	**la moto acuática**	*la moto akwateeka*
journey	**el viaje**	*el byahe*
July	**julio**	*hoolyo*

| **June** | junio | *hoonyo* |

In June, the Fiesta de **San Juan** brightens many towns and
villages with fireworks, bonfires, music and dancing all night.

| junction | **el cruce** | *el kroothe* |
| just (only) | **sólo** | *solo* |

K

to keep	**guardar**	*gwardar*
key	**la llave**	*la yabe*
keyboard	**el teclado**	*el teklado*
key ring	**el llavero**	*el yabero*
kid	**el/la crío/a**	*el/la kreeo/a*
to kill	**matar**	*matar*
kind (nice)	**amable**	*amable*

kind (sort)	**la clase**	*la klase*
kiosk	**el quiosco**	*el kyosko*
kiss	**el beso**	*el beso*
to kiss	**besar**	*besar*
to knock	**golpear**	*golpear*
to know (person)	**conocer**	*konother*
to know (knowledge)	**saber**	*saber*

L

label	**la etiqueta**	*la eteeketta*
ladies (toilets)	**los servicios de señoras**	*los serbeethyos de senyoras*
lady	**la señora**	*la senyora*
language	**el idioma**	*el eedeeoma*
last	**último/a**	*el oolteemo/a*
late (delayed)	**retrasado**	*retrasado*
late (time)	**tarde**	*tarde*
launderette	**la lavandería**	*la labandereea*
lawyer	**el/la abogado**	*el/la abogado*
to leave	**salir**	*saleer*
left	**la izquierda**	*la eethkyerda*
less	**menos**	*menos*
letter	**la carta**	*la karta*
library	**la biblioteca**	*la beeblyoteka*
lifeguard	**el/la socorrista**	*el/la sokorreesta*
life jacket	**el chaleco salvavidas**	*el chaleco salbabeedas*
lift	**el ascensor**	*el asthendor*
to like	**gustar**	*goostar*
to listen to	**escuchar**	*eskoochar*
little (a little)	**un poco**	*oon poko*
local	**local**	*lokal*
to look	**mirar**	*meerar*
to lose	**perder**	*perder*
lost property	**los objetos perdidos**	*los obhetos perdeedos*
luggage	**el equipaje**	*el ekeepahe*

M

madam	**la señora**	*la senyora*
mail	**el correo**	*el korreo*
main	**principal**	*preentheepal*
to make	**hacer**	*ather*
man	**el hombre**	*el ombre*
manager	**el/la director/a**	*el/la deerektor/a*
many	**muchos/as**	*moochos/as*
map (city)	**el plano**	*el plano*
map (road)	**el mapa**	*el mapa*

| **March** | **marzo** | *martho* |

Valencia is worth a visit in March when the big **fiesta** of fire, **Las Fallas**, burns bright.

market	**el mercado**	*el merkado*
married	**casado/a**	*kasado/a*
May	**mayo**	*mayo*
maybe	**quizás**	*keethas*

mechanic	**el/la mecánico/a**	*el/la mekaneeko/a*
to meet	**encontrar**	*enkontrar*
meeting	**la reunión**	*la reoonyon*
message	**el recado**	*el rekado*
midday	**el mediodía**	*el medyodeea*
midnight	**la medianoche**	*la medyanoche*
minimum	**mínimo/a**	*meeneemo/a*
minute	**el minuto**	*el meenooto*
to miss (a person)	**echar de menos**	*echar de menos*
to miss (a train)	**perder**	*perder*
missing	**desaparecido/a**	*desaparetheedo/a*
mobile phone	**el teléfono móvil**	*el telephono mobil*
moment	**el momento**	*el momento*
money	**el dinero**	*el deenero*
more	**más**	*mas*
mosquito	**el mosquito**	*el moskeeto*
most	**la mayoría**	*la mayoreea*
mother	**la madre**	*la madre*
much	**mucho**	*moocho*
museum	**el museo**	*el mooseo*
musical	**el musical**	*el mooseekal*
must	**tener que**	*tener ke*
my	**mi**	*mee*

N

name	**el nombre**	*el nombre*
nationality	**la nacionalidad**	*la nathyonalidath*
near	**cerca (de)**	*therka*
necessary	**necesario/a**	*nethesaryo/a*
to need	**necesitar**	*netheseetar*
never	**nunca**	*noonka*
new	**nuevo/a**	*nwebo/a*
news	**las noticias**	*las noteethyas*
newspaper	**el periódico**	*el peryodeeko*
next	**el/la siguiente**	*el/la seegyente*
next to	**al lado de**	*al lado de*
nice (people)	**simpático/a**	*seempateeko/a*
nice (things)	**bonito/a**	*boneeto/a*
night	**la noche**	*la noche*
nightclub	**la sala de fiestas**	*la sala de fyestas*
north	**el norte**	*el norte*
note (money)	**el billete**	*el beeyete*
nothing	**nada**	*nada*
November	**noviembre**	*nobyembre*
now	**ahora**	*aora*
nowhere	**en ningún sitio**	*en neengoon seeteeo*

| **nudist beach** | la playa nudista | *la playa noodeesta* |

Nudism is legal in today's Spain. Naturist resorts and beaches have, over the recent years, become more popular.

| number | **el número** | *el noomero* |

O

| object | **el objeto** | *el obheto* |

October	**octubre**	*oktoobre*
off (food)	**malo/a**	*malo/a*
off (switched)	**apagado/a**	*apagado/a*
office	**la oficina**	*la opheetheena*
OK	**de acuerdo**	*de akwerdo*
on	**en**	*en*
once	**una vez**	*oona beth*
only	**sólo**	*solo*
open	**abierto/a**	*abyerto/a*
to open	**abrir**	*abreer*
operator	**el/la telefonista**	*el/la telephoneesta*
opposite (place)	**enfrente (de)**	*enphrente (de)*
optician's	**la óptica**	*la opteeka*
or	**o**	*o*
to order	**pedir**	*pedeer*
other	**otro/a**	*otro/a*
out of order	**estropeado/a**	*estropeado/a*
outdoor	**al aire libre**	*al ayre leebre*
outside	**fuera (de)**	*phwera (de)*
overnight	**por la noche**	*por la noche*
owner	**el/la dueño/a**	*el/la dwenyo/a*
oxygen	**el oxígeno**	*el okseeheno*

P

painkiller	**el calmante**	*el kalmante*
pair	**el par**	*el par*
parents	**los padres**	*los padres*
park	**el parque**	*el parke*
to park	**aparcar**	*aparkar*
parking	**el aparcamiento**	*el aparkamyento*
party	**la fiesta**	*le fyesta*
passport	**el pasaporte**	*el pasaporte*
to pay	**pagar**	*pagar*
people	**la gente**	*la hente*
perhaps	**quizás**	*keethas*
person	**la persona**	*la persona*
phone	**el teléfono**	*el telephono*
to phone	**llamar por teléfono**	*yamar por telephono*
photo	**la foto**	*la photo*
phrase book	**la guía de conversación**	*la geea de konbersathyon*
place	**el lugar**	*el loogar*
platform	**el andén**	*el anden*
police	**la policía**	*la poleetheea*
port (drink)	**el oporto**	*el oporto*
port (sea)	**el puerto**	*el pwerto*
possible	**posible**	*poseeble*
post	**el correo**	*el korreo*
post office	**la oficina de correos**	*la opheetheena korreos*
to prefer	**preferir**	*prefeereer*
prescription	**la receta**	*la retheta*
pretty	**bonito/a**	*boneeto/a*
price	**el precio**	*el prethyo*
private	**privado/a**	*preebado/a*
probably	**probablemente**	*probablemente*

problem	el problema	el problema
pub	el pub / el bar	el poob / el bar
public transport	el transporte público	el transporte poobleeko
to put	poner	poner

Q

quality	la calidad	la kaleedath
quantity	la cantidad	la kanteedath
quarter	el cuarto	el kwarto
query	la pregunta	la pregoonta
question	la pregunta	la pregoonta

queue	la cola	la cola

Queuing is not really a virtue of the Spanish. Do as the locals do.

quick	rápido/a	rapeedo/a
quickly	de prisa	de preesa
quiet	tranquilo/a	trankeelo/a
quite	bastante	bastante
quiz	el consurso	el konkoorso

R

radio	la radio	la radyo
railway	el ferrocarril	el pherrokarryl
rain	la lluvia	la yoobya
rape	la violación	la beeolathyon
razor blade	la hoja de afeitar	la oha de aphaytar
ready	listo/a	leesto/a
real	real	real
receipt	el recibo	el retheebo
to receive	recibir	retheebeer
reception	la recepción	la rethepthyon
receptionist	el/la recepcionista	el/la rethepthyoneesta
to recommend	recomendar	rekomendar
reduction	el descuento	el deskwento
refund	el reembolso	el re-embolso
to refuse	negarse	negarse
to relax	relajarse	relaharse
rent	el alquiler	el alkeeler
to rent	alquilar	alkeelar
to request	pedir	pedeer
reservation	la reserva	la reserba
to reserve	reservar	reserbar
retired	jubilado/a	hoobeelado/a
rich	rico/a	reeko/a

to ride	montar a caballo	montar ah kabayo

For an adventure holiday, explore southern Spain on the back of a purebred Andalusian horse.

right	la derecha	la derecha
to be right	tener razón	tener rathon
to ring	llamar	yamar
road	la carretera	la karretera

to rob	**robar**	*robar*
room	**la habitación**	*la abeetathyon*
route	**la ruta**	*la roota*
rude	**grosero/a**	*grosero/a*
ruins	**las ruinas**	*las rooeenas*
to run	**correr**	*korrer*

S

safe	**seguro/a**	*segooro/a*
sauna	**la sauna**	*la saona*
Scotland	**Escocia**	*eskothya*
Scottish	**escocés/esa**	*eskothes/esa*
sea	**el mar**	*el mar*
seat	**el asiento**	*al asyento*
seat belt	**el cinturón de seguridad**	*el theentooron de segooreedath*
sedative	**el sedante**	*el sedante*
see you later	**hasta luego**	*asta lwego*
self-service	**el autoservicio**	*el awtoserbeethyo*
to sell	**vender**	*bender*
to send	**enviar**	*enbyar*
sensible	**sensato/a**	*sensato/a*
September	**septiembre**	*setyembre*
to serve	**servir**	*serbeer*
service	**el servicio**	*el serbeethyo*
shop	**la tienda**	*la tyenda*
shopping	**las compras**	*las kompras*
shopping centre	**el centro comercial**	*el thentro komerthyal*
short	**corto/a**	*korto/a*
show	**el espectáculo**	*el espektakoolo*
to show	**mostrar**	*mostrar*
shut	**cerrado/a**	*therrado/a*
sign	**la señal**	*la senyal*
to sign	**firmar**	*feermar*
signature	**la firma**	*la feerma*
since	**desde**	*desde*
sir	**el señor**	*el senyor*
sister	**la hermana**	*la ermana*

| **ski** | **el esquí** | *el eskee* |

Visit the Sierra Nevada for a skiing holiday and make a side trip to nearby Granada, just 30 miles away.

to sleep	**dormir**	*dormeer*
sleeping pill	**el somnífero**	*el somneephero*
slow	**despacio**	*despathyo*
small	**pequeño/a**	*pekenyo/a*
to smoke	**fumar**	*foomar*
soft	**suave**	*sooabe*
some	**algunos/as**	*algoonos/as*
something	**algo**	*algo*
son	**el hijo**	*el eeho*
soon	**pronto**	*pronto*
south	**el sur**	*el soor*
South Africa	**Sudáfrica**	*soodaphreeka*

South African	sudafricano/a	soodaphreekano/a
Spain	España	espanya
Spanish	español/a	espanyol/a
speed	la velocidad	la belotheedath
to spell	deletrear	deletrear
sport	el deporte	el deporte
stadium	el estadio	el estadyo
staff	el personal	personal
stamp	el sello	el seyo
to start	empezar	empethar
to start (car)	poner en marcha	poner en marcha
station	la estación	la estathyon
pound sterling	la libra esterlina	la leebra esterleena
to stop	parar	parar
straight	recto/a	rekto/a
street	la calle	la kaye
stress	el estrés	el estres
suddenly	de repente	de repente
suitcase	la maleta	la maletta
sun	el sol	el sol
sunglasses	las gafas de sol	las gaphas de sol
surname	el apellido	el apeyeedo
swimming pool	la piscina	la peestheena
symptom	el síntoma	el seentoma

T

table	la mesa	la mesa
to take	tomar	tomar
tall	alto/a	alto/a
tampons	los tampones	los tampones
tax	el impuesto	el eempooesto
tax free	libre de impuestos	leebre de eempooestos
taxi	el taxi	el taksee
taxi rank	la parada de taxis	la parada de taksees
telephone	el teléfono	el telephono
telephone box	la cabina de teléfono	la kabeena de tele-phono
television	la televisión	la telebeesyon
tennis	el tenis	el tenees
tennis court	la pista de tenis	la peesta de tenees
terrace	la terraza	la terratha
to text	mandar un mensaje al móvil	mandar un mensahe al mobeel
that	ese/a	ese/a
theft	el robo	el robo
then	entonces	entonthes
there	allí	ayee
thing	la cosa	la kosa
to think	pensar	pensar
thirsty	sediento/a	sedyento/a
this	este/a	este/a
through	a través	a trabes
ticket (bus)	el billete	el beeyete
ticket (cinema)	la entrada	la entrada
ticket (parking)	la multa	la moolta

ticket (shopping)	**el recibo**	*el retheebo*
ticket office	**la taquilla**	*la takeeya*
time	**el tiempo**	*el tyempo*
time (clock)	**la hora**	*la ora*
timetable	**el horario**	*el oraryo*

| **tip (money)** | **la propina** | *la propeena* |

Tipping is the norm, but not obligatory. Five to ten per cent of the restaurant bill is appropriate.

tired	**cansado/a**	*kansado/a*
to	**a**	*ah*
tobacco	**el tabaco**	*el tabako*
today	**hoy**	*oy*
toilet	**el servicio**	*el serbeethyo*
toiletries	**los artículos de baño**	*los arteekoolos de banyo*
toll	**el peaje**	*el peahe*
tomorrow	**mañana**	*manyana*
tonight	**esta noche**	*esta noche*
too	**también**	*tambyen*
tourist office	**la oficina de turismo**	*la opheetheena de tooreesmo*
town	**la ciudad**	*la theeoodath*
town hall	**el ayuntamiento**	*el ayoontamyento*

| **train** | **el tren** | *el tren* |

The new high-speed train AVE races between Madrid and Seville in just two and a half hours.

tram	**el tranvía**	*el trambeea*
to translate	**traducir**	*tradootheer*
travel	**el viaje**	*el beeahe*
travel agency	**la agencia de viajes**	*le ahenthya de beeahes*
true	**verdadero/a**	*berdadero/a*
typical	**típico/a**	*teepeeko/a*

U

ugly	**feo/a**	*feo/a*
ulcer	**la úlcera**	*la oolthera*
umbrella	**el paraguas**	*el paragwas*
uncomfortable	**incómodo/a**	*eenkomodo/a*
unconcious	**inconsciente**	*eenkonsthyente*
under	**debajo (de)**	*debaho (de)*
underground (tube)	**el metro**	*el metro*
to understand	**entender**	*entender*
underwear	**la ropa interior**	*la ropa eenteryor*
unemployed	**desempleado/a**	*desempleado/a*
unpleasant	**desagradable**	*desagradable*
up	**arriba**	*areeba*
upstairs	**arriba**	*areeba*
urgent	**urgente**	*oorhente*
to use	**usar**	*oosar*
useful	**útil**	*ooteel*
usually	**normalmente**	*normalmente*

V

vacant	libre	*leebre*
vacation	las vacaciones	*las bakathyones*
vaccination	la vacuna	*la bakoona*
valid	válido/a	*baleedo/a*
valuables	los objetos de valor	*los obhetos de balor*
value	el valor	*el balor*
VAT	el IVA	*el eeba*
vegetarian	vegetariano/a	*behetaryano/a*
vehicle	el vehículo	*el beheekoolo*
very	muy	*mooy*
visa	el visado	*el beesado*
visit	la visita	*la beeseeta*
to visit	visitar	*beeseetar*
vitamin	la vitamina	*la beetameena*
to vomit	vomitar	*bomeetar*

W

waiter/waitress	el/la camarero/a	*el/la kamarero/a*
waiting room	la sala de espera	*la sala de espera*
Wales	Gales	*hales*
to walk	caminar	*kameenar*

wallet	**la cartera**	***la kartera***

Take care of your wallet! Pickpocketing is one of the most common crimes, especially in the cities.

to want	querer	*kerer*
to wash	lavar	*labar*
watch	el reloj	*el reloh*
to watch	mirar	*meerar*
water	agua	*agwa*
water sports	los deportes acuáticos	*los deportes agwateekos*
way (manner)	la manera	*la manera*
way (route)	el camino	*el kameeno*
way in	la entrada	*la entrada*
way out	la salida	*la saleeda*
weather	el tiempo	*el tyempo*
web	la internet	*la eenternet*
website	la página web	*la paheena web*
week	la semana	*la semana*
weekday	el día laborable	*el deea laborable*
weekend	el fin de semana	*el feen de semana*
welcome	bienvenido/a	*byenbeneedo/a*
well	bien	*byen*
Welsh	galés/esa	*hales/esa*
west	el oeste	*el oeste*
what?	¿qué?	*keh?*
wheelchair	la silla de ruedas	*sa seeya de rooedas*
when?	¿cuándo?	*kwando?*
where?	¿dónde?	*dondeh?*
which?	¿cuál?	*kwal?*
while	mientras	*myentras*
who?	¿quién?	*kyen?*

why?	¿por qué?	por keh?
wife	la esposa	la esposa
to win	ganar	ganar
with	con	kon
without	sin	seen
woman	la mujer	la mooher
wonderful	maravilloso/a	marabeeyoso/a
word	la palabra	la palabra
work	el trabajo	el trabaho
to work (machine)	funcionar	foonthyonar
to work (person)	trabajar	trabahar
world	el mundo	el moondo
worried	preocupado/a	preokoopado/a
worse	peor	peor
to write	escribir	eskreebeer
wrong (mistaken)	equivocado/a	ekeebokado/a

X

xenophobe	xenófobo/a	ksenophobo/a
xenophobia	la xenofobia	la ksenophobeea
x-ray	la radiografía	la radyographeea
to x-ray	hacer una radiografía	ather oona radyographeea
x-rays	los rayos X	los rayos ekees

Y

yacht	el yate	el yate
year	el año	el anyo
yearly	anual	anooal
yellow pages	las páginas amarillas	las paheenas amareeyas
yes	sí	see
yesterday	ayer	ayer
yet	todavía	todabeea
you (formal)	usted	oosteth
you (informal)	tú	too
young	joven	hoben
your (formal)	su/s	soo/s
your (informal)	tu/s	too/s
youth hostel	el albergue juvenil	el alberge hoobeneel

Z

zebra crossing	el paso de cebra	el paso de thebra
zero	el cero	el thero
zip	la cremallera	la kremayera
zone	la zona	la thona
zoo	el zoo	el tho

A

a	*ah*	to
a través	*a trabes*	through
abajo	*abaho*	down
abierto/a	*abyerto/a*	open
abogado/a, el/la	*el/la abogado/a*	lawyer
abril	*abreel*	April
abrir	*abreer*	to open
accidente, el	*el aktheedente*	accident
aduana, la	*la adooana*	customs

aeropuerto, el	*el aeropooerto*	airport

Thirty main airports, spread across the country, allow visitors to reach every corner of Spain quickly and conveniently.

agencia de viajes, la	*la ahenthya de beeahes*	travel agency
agosto	*agosto*	August
agua, el	*el agwa*	water
ahora	*aora*	now
al lado de	*al lado de*	next to
al menos	*al menos*	at least
alarma, la	*la alarma*	alarm
alarma de incendios, la	*la alarma de eenthendyos*	fire alarm

albergue juvenil, el	*el alberge hoobeneel*	youth hostel

Select one of Spain's many youth hostels and book online at www.reaj.com/index_en.html.

alergia, la	*la alerhya*	allergy
algo	*algo*	something
alguno/a (s)	*algoono/a(s)*	any, some
allí	*ayee*	there
alojamiento, el	*el alohamyento*	accommodation
alquilar	*alkeelar*	to rent
alquiler, el	*el alkeeler*	rent
alrededor	*alrededor*	around
alto/a	*alto/a*	tall
amable (nice)	*amable*	kind
ambulancia, la	*la amboolanthya*	ambulance
América	*amereeka*	America
americano/a	*amereekano/a*	American
amigo/a, el/la	*el/la ameego/a*	friend
amueblado/a	*amooeblado/a*	furnished
andén, el	*el anden*	platform
aniversario, el	*el aneebersaryo*	anniversary
año, el	*el anyo*	year
antes (de)	*antes (de)*	before
anual	*anooal*	yearly

apagado/a	*apagado/a*	switched off
aparcamiento, el	*el aparkamyento*	parking
aparcar	*aparkar*	to park
apartamento, el	*el apartamento*	apartment
apellido, el	*el apeyeedo*	surname
aquí	*akee*	here
área, el	*el areya*	area
arriba	*areeba*	up
arte, el	*el arte*	art
ascensor, el	*el asthensor*	lift
asiento, el	*el asyento*	seat
aspirina, la	*la aspeereena*	aspirin
atacar	*atakar*	to attack
atención, la	*la atenthyon*	attention
atrás(place)	*atras*	back
Australia	*awstralya*	Australia
australiano/a	*awstralyano/a*	Australian
autobús, el	*el awtoboos*	bus
autoservicio, el	*el awtoserbeethyo*	self-service
avión, el	*el abyon*	aeroplane
ayer	*ayer*	yesterday
ayudar	*ayoodar*	to help
ayuntamiento, el	*el ayoontamyento*	town hall

B

bahía, la (coast)	*la baeea*	bay
baño, el	*el banyo*	bath
bar, el (pub)	*el bar*	bar
barato/a	*barato/a*	cheap
barbacoa, la	*la barbakoa*	barbecue
barrio, el	*el baryo*	neighbourhood
bastante	*bastante*	enough
bebé, el	*el bebeh*	baby
beber	*beber*	to drink
besar	*besar*	to kiss
beso, el	*el beso*	kiss
biblioteca, la	*la beeblyoteka*	library
bicicleta, la	*la beetheekletta*	bicycle
bien	*byen*	well
bien hecho	*byen echo*	well done
bienvenido/a	*byenbeneedo/a*	welcome
billete, el (money)	*el beeyete*	note
billete, el (bus)	*el beeyete*	ticket
blando/a	*blando/a*	soft
bodega, la	*la bodega*	wine cellar, restaurant
bolsa, la	*la bolsa*	bag
bonito/a (things)	*boneeto/a*	nice
bonito/a (people)	*boneeto/a*	pretty
bosque, el	*el boske*	forest
bote, el	*el bote*	boat
botella, la	*la boteya*	bottle
bronceador, el	*el brontheador*	suntan lotion
bueno/a	*bweno/a*	good
bufé, el	*el boophe*	buffet

buscar	*booskar*	to look for
butacas, las (theatre)	*las bootakas*	stalls
buzón, el	*el boothon*	postbox

C

cabina de teléfono, la	*la kabeena de telephono*	phone box
cafetería, la	*la kaphetereea*	café
cajero automático, el	*el kahero awtomateeko*	cash point
calculadora, la	*la kalkooladora*	calculator
calidad, la	*la kaleedath*	quality
caliente	*kalyente*	hot
calle, la	*la kaye*	street
calle principal, la	*la kaye preentheepal*	high street
calmante, el	*el kalmante*	painkiller
calor, el	*el kalor*	heat
cámara fotográfica, la	*la kamara photographeeka*	camera
camarero/a, el/la	*el/la kamarero/a*	waiter/tress
cambiar	*kambyar*	to change
cambio, el	*el kambeeo*	exchange rate
caminar	*kameenar*	to walk

camino, el	*el kameeno*	**way** (route)

Every year thousands of people make the pilgrimage to Santiago de Compostela – on foot.

campo, el	*el kampo*	countryside
campo de golf, el	*el kampo de golf*	golf course
cancelar	*kanthelar*	to cancel
cansado/a	*kansado/a*	tired
cantidad, la	*la kanteedath*	quantity
carnet de identidad, el	*el karneh de eedenteedath*	identity card
carrete, el (camera)	*el karrete*	film
carretera, la	*la karretera*	road
carta, la	*la karta*	letter
cartera, la	*la kartera*	wallet
casado/a	*kasado/a*	married
casino, el	*el kaseeno*	casino
catedral, la	*la katedral*	cathedral
cd, el	*el thedeh*	CD
centro, el	*el thentro*	centre
centro comercial, el	*el thentro komerthyal*	shopping centre
cerca	*therka*	near
cerca de	*therka de*	close by
cero, el	*el thero*	zero
cerrado/a	*therrado/a*	closed
cerrar	*therrar*	to close
chaleco salvavidas, el	*el chaleco salbabeedas*	life jacket
cheque, el	*el chekeh*	cheque
chica, la	*la cheeka*	girl
chico, el	*el cheeko*	boy

ciclismo, el	el theekleesmo	cycling
cigarrillo, el	el theegareeyo	cigarette
cine, el	el theene	cinema
cinturón de seguridad, el	el theentooron de segooreedath	seat belt
cita, la	la theeta	appointment

| **ciudad, la** | **la theeoodath** | **city, town** |

Madrid is Spain's largest city; 5.5m people live in its metropolitan area.

clase, la (sort)	la klase	kind
clase preferente, la	la klase prepherente	business class
cliente, el	el klyente	customer
club, el	el kloob	club
cobrar	kobrar	to charge
coche, el	el koche	car
cola, la	la cola	queue
color, el	el kolor	colour
comedor, el	el komedor	dining room
comer	komer	to eat
¿cómo?	komo?	how?
comprar	komprar	to buy
compras, las	las kompras	shopping
compresa, la	le kompresa	sanitary towel
con	kon	with
conducir	kondootheer	to drive
conductor/a, el/la	el/la kondooktor/a	driver
confirmación, la	la konpheermathyon	confirmation
confirmar	konpheermar	to confirm
conocer (person)	konother	to know
consulado, el	el konsoolado	consulate
consurso, el	el konkoorso	quiz
contagioso/a	kontahyoso/a	contagious
correo, el	el korreo	mail, post
correo aéreo, el	el korreo aereo	airmail
correo electrónico, el	el korreo elektroneeko	e-mail
correr	korrer	to run
corrida de toros, la	la korreeda de torros	bullfight
cortar	kortar	to cut
corte, el	el korte	cut
corto/a	korto/a	short
cosa, la	la kosa	thing
costa, la	la kosta	coast
costar	kostar	to cost
crema, la	la krema	cream
crema de afeitar, la	la krema de afaytar	shaving cream
crema para después del sol, la	la krema para despwes del sol	after-sun lotion
cremallera, la	la kremayera	zip
crío/a, el/la	el/la kreeo/a	kid
cruce, el	el kroothe	junction
¿cuál?	kwal?	which?

¿cuándo?	*kwando?*	when?
¿cuánto?	*kwanto?*	how much?
¿cuánto tiempo?	*kwanto tyempo?*	how long?
cuarto, el	*el kwarto*	quarter
cuenta, la	*la kwenta*	bill
cuna, la	*la koona*	cot

D

daño/s, el/los	*el/los danyo/s*	damage
dar	*dar*	to give
de / desde	*de / desde*	from
de acuerdo	*de akwerdo*	OK
de prisa	*de preesa*	quickly
¡de prisa!	*de preesa!*	hurry up!
de repente	*de repente*	suddenly
debajo (de)	*debaho (de)*	below
deletrear	*deletrear*	to spell
delito, el	*el deleeto*	crime
dentro (de)	*dentro (de)*	inside
dependiente/a, el/la	*el/la dependyente/a*	shop assistant
deporte, el	*el deporte*	sport
deportes acuáticos, los	*los deportes agwateekos*	water sports
derecha, la	*la derecha*	right
desagradable	*desagradable*	unpleasant
desaparecido/a	*desaparetheedo/a*	missing
descuento, el	*el deskwento*	discount
desde	*desde*	since
desempleado/a	*desempleado/a*	unemployed
desidratar	*deseedratar*	to dehydrate
desinfectante, el	*el deseenphektante*	disinfectant
despacio	*despathyo*	slow
después	*despwes*	after
detrás (de)	*detras (de)*	behind
día, el	*el deea*	day
día laborable, el	*el deea laborable*	weekday
diciembre	*deethyembre*	December
difícil	*deepheethyl*	difficult
dinero, el	*el deenero*	money
dinero en efectivo, el	*el deenero en ephekteebo*	cash
director/a, el/la	*el/la deerektor/a*	manager
discapacitado/a	*deeskapatheetado/a*	disable
discoteca, la	*la deeskoteka*	disco
disponible	*deesponeeble*	available
divertirse	*deeberteerse*	to enjoy
doble	*doble*	double
doler	*doler*	to hurt
¿dónde?	*dondeh?*	where?
dormir	*dormeer*	to sleep
drogas, las	*las drogas*	drugs
ducha, la	*la doocha*	shower
dueño/a, el/la	*el/la dwenyo/a*	owner
durante	*doorante*	during

echar de menos (a person)	*echar de menos*	to miss

embajada, la	*la embahada*	embassy

The British Embassy is located in Madrid, with consular offices in Barcelona, Málaga and various other towns.

emergencia, la	*la emerhenthya*	emergency
empezar	*empethar*	to start
en	*en*	in, on, at
en avión	*en abyon*	by plane
en casa	*en kasa*	at home
en ningún sitio	*en neengoon see-teeo*	nowhere
encontrar	*enkontrar*	to meet
enero	*enero*	January
enfermo/a	*enfermo/a*	ill
enfrente (de) (place)	*enphrente (de)*	opposite
¡enhorabuena!	*enorabwena!*	congratulations!
entender	*entender*	to understand
entonces	*entonthes*	then
entrada, la (cinema)	*la entrada*	ticket
entrada, la (place)	*la entrada*	way in
entre	*entre*	between
enviar	*enbyar*	to send
equipaje, el	*el ekeepahe*	luggage
equivocado/a	*ekeebokado/a*	mistaken
error, el	*el error*	error
escaleras, las	*las eskaleras*	stairs
escasez, la	*la eskaseth*	shortage
escocés/esa	*eskothes/esa*	Scottish
Escocia	*eskothya*	Scotland
escribir	*eskreebeer*	to write

escuchar	*eskoochar*	to listen to

Several **flamenco** festivals around the country provide a great opportunity to experience this quintessentially Spanish tradition.

ese/a	*ese/a*	that
España	*espanya*	Spain
español/a	*espanyol/a*	Spanish
espectáculo, el	*el espektakoolo*	show
esposa, la	*la esposa*	wife
esquí, el	*el eskee*	ski
estación, la	*la estathyon*	station
estación de autobuses, la	*la estathyon de awtobooses*	bus station
estadio, el	*el estadyo*	stadium
estanco, el	*el estanko*	tobacconists'
este/a	*este/a*	this
estrés, el	*el estres*	stress
estropeado/a	*estropeado/a*	out of order
etiqueta, la	*la eteeketta*	label

exactamente	*eksaktamente*	exactly
exportar	*eksportar*	to export
exposición, la	*la eksposeethyon*	exhibition

F

facturar (airport)	*phaktoorar*	to check in
favorito/a	*faboreeto/a*	favourite
febrero	*febrero*	February
fecha, la (calendar)	*la phecha*	date
feo/a	*feo/a*	ugly
ferrocarril, el	*el pherrokarryl*	railway
fiesta, la	*la fyesta*	holiday, party
fin de semana, el	*el feen de semana*	weekend
firma, la	*la feerma*	signature
firmar	*feermar*	to sign
foto, la	*la photo*	photo
fresco/a	*phresko/a*	cool
frío/a	*phreeo/a*	cold
fuego, el	*el phooego*	fire
fuera (de)	*phwera (de)*	outside
fumar	*foomar*	to smoke
funcionar (machine)	*foonthyonar*	to work

fútbol, el	*el phootbol*	football

Visit the Santiago Bernabeu football stadium in
Madrid on a guided tour or – even better – when the
home team is playing.

G

gafas, las	*las gaphas*	glasses
gafas de sol, las	*las gaphas de sol*	sunglasses
galería, la	*la galereea*	gallery
Gales	*hales*	Wales
galés/esa	*hales/esa*	Welsh
ganar	*ganar*	to win
garage, el	*el garahe*	garage
garantía, la	*la garanteea*	guarantee
gas, el	*el gas*	gas
gasolinera, la	*la gasoleenera*	filling station
gente, la	*la hente*	people
golf, el	*el golph*	golf
golpear	*golpear*	to knock
gorro de baño, el	*el gorro de banyo*	bathing cap
grande	*grande*	big
gratis (money)	*gratees*	free
gripe, la	*la greepe*	flu
grosero/a	*grosero/a*	rude
grupo, el	*el groopo*	group
guardar	*gwardar*	to keep
guía, la	*la geea*	guide
guía de conversación, la	*la geea de konbersathyon*	phrase book
gustar	*goostar*	to like

H

habitación, la	la abeetathyon	room
hace	athe	ago
hacer	ather	to make
hacer una radiografía	ather oona radyographeea	to x-ray
hermana, la	la ermana	sister
hermano, el	el ermano	brother
hija, la	la eeha	daughter
hijo, el	el eeho	son
hoja de afeitar, la	la oha de aphaytar	razor blade
hombre, el	el ombre	man
homosexual	omoseksooal	homosexual
hora, la (clock)	la ora	timex
horario, el	el oraryo	timetable
hospital, el	el ospeetal	hospital
hoy	oy	today

I

| **idioma, el** | **el eedeeoma** | **language** |

The Spaniards aren't the best at learning foreign languages. Better practise your Spanish phrases!

iglesia, la	la eeglesya	church
importante	eemportante	important
importar	eemportar	to import
impreso, el (document)	el eempreso	form
impuesto, el	el eempooesto	tax
impuestos, los (tax)	los eempooestos	duty
incómodo/a	eenkomodo/a	uncomfortable
inconsciente	eenkonsthyente	unconcious
información, la	la eenphormathyon	information
Inglaterra	eenglaterra	England
inglés/esa	eengles/esa	English
inmediatamente	eenmedyatamente	immediately
instalaciones, las	las eenstalathyones	facilities
instrucciones, las	las eenstrookthyones	directions
interesante	eenteresante	interesting
internacional	eenternathyonal	international
internet, la	la eenternet	web
intoxicación alimenticia, la	la eentokseekathyon aleementeethya	food poisoning
ir	eer	to go
Irlanda	eerlanda	Ireland
irlandés/esa	eerlandes/esa	Irish

| **isla, la** | **la eesla** | **island** |

The Islas Balearas (Balearics) not only draw the crowds with 300 days of sunshine a year, but also for their diversity, ancient history and traditions.

itinerario, el	el eeteeneraryo	itinerary
IVA, el	el eeba	VAT
izquierda, la	la eethkyerda	left

J

joven	hoben	young
jubilado/a	hoobeelado/a	retired
julio	hoolyo	July
junio	hoonyo	June

K

kilo, el	el keelo	kilo
kilometraje, el	el keelometrahe	mileage
kiosko, el	el keeosko	newsstand

L

lavandería, la	la labandereea	launderette
lavar	labar	to wash
lavar en seco	labar en sekko	to dry clean
lejos	lehos	far
lentillas, las	las lenteeyas	contact lenses
libra esterlina, la	la leebra esterleena	pound sterling
libre	leebre	free, vacant
libre de impuestos	leebre de eem-pooestos	tax free
libro, el	el leebro	book
listo/a	leesto/a	ready
llamar	yamar	to call
llamar por teléfono	yamar por telephono	to phone
llave, la	la yabe	key
llavero, el	el yabero	key ring
llegada, la	la yegada	arrival
lluvia, la	la yoobya	rain
local	lokal	local
lugar, el	el loogar	place

M

madre, la	la madre	mother
maleta, la	la maletta	suitcase
malo/a (food)	malo/a	off
mañana	manyana	tomorrow
mancha, la	la mancha	stain
mandar por fax	mandar por phaks	to fax
mandar un mensaje al móvil	mandar un mensahe al mobeel	to text
manera, la	la manera	manner
mapa, el	el mapa	map (road)
mar, el	el mar	sea
maravilloso/a	marabeeyoso/a	wonderful
marcar	markar	to dial
marido, el	el mareedo	husband
marzo	martho	March
más	mas	more

matar   *ma**tar***   to kill
Like it or not, the moment the **matador** kills the bull
in the **corrida de toros** is breathtaking.

mayo	*mayo*	May
mayoría, la	*la mayoreea*	most
mecánico/a, el/la	*el/la mekaneeko/a*	mechanic
medianoche, la	*la medyanoche*	midnight
medicina, la	*la medeetheena*	drug
médico/a, el/la	*el/la medeeko/a*	doctor
medio/a	*medeeo/a*	half
mediodía, el	*el medyodeea*	midday
medusa, la	*la medoosa*	jellyfish
mejor	*mehor*	better
mejor, el/la/lo	*el/la/lo mehor*	the best
menos	*menos*	less
mercado, el	*el merkado*	market
mesa, la	*la mesa*	table
metro, el (tube)	*el metro*	underground
mi	*mee*	my
mientras	*myentras*	while
mínimo/a	*meeneemo/a*	minimum
minuto, el	*el meenooto*	minute
mirar	*meerar*	to look
molestar	*molestar*	to disturb
momento, el	*el momento*	moment
moneda, la	*la moneda*	currency
montar a caballo	*montar ah kabayo*	to ride a horse
mosquito, el	*el moskeeto*	mosquito
mostrar	*mostrar*	to show
moto acuática, la	*la moto akwateeka*	jet ski
mucho	*moocho*	much
muchos/as	*moochos/as*	many
mujer, la	*la mooher*	woman
multa, la (parking)	*la moolta*	ticket
mundo, el	*el moondo*	world

museo, el   *el mooseo*   museum
In 2004 the city of Málaga, birthplace of Pablo
Picasso, inaugurated the Museo Picasso Málaga.

musical, el	*el mooseekal*	musical
muy	*mooy*	very

N

nacionalidad, la	*la nathyonalidath*	nationality
nada	*nada*	nothing
necesario/a	*nethesaryo/a*	necessary
necesitar	*netheseetar*	to need
negarse	*negarse*	to refuse
negocio, el	*el negothyo*	business
niño/a, el/la	*el/la neenyo/a*	child
noche, la	*la noche*	night
nombre, el	*el nombre*	name

normalmente	*normalmente*	usually
norte, el	*el norte*	north
noticias, las	*las noteethyas*	news
noviembre	*nobyembre*	November
nuevo/a	*nwebo/a*	new
número, el	*el noomero*	number
nunca	*noonka*	never

O

o	*o*	or
objeto, el	*el obheto*	object
objetos de valor, los	*los obhetos de balor*	valuables
objetos perdidos, los	*los obhetos perdeedos*	lost property
obtener	*obtener*	to get
octubre	*oktoobre*	October
oeste, el	*el oeste*	west
oficina, la	*la opheetheena*	office
oficina de cambio, la	*la opheetheena de kambyo*	bureau de change
oficina de correos, la	*la opheetheena de korreos*	post office
oficina de turismo, la	*la opheetheena de tooreesmo*	tourist office
oporto, el (drink)	*el oporto*	port
óptica, la	*la opteeka*	opticians'
organizar	*organeethar*	to arrange
otra vez	*otra beth*	again
otro/a	*otro/a*	other
otro/a (s)	*otro/a (s)*	another
oxígeno, el	*el okseeheno*	oxygen

P

padre, el	*el padre*	father
padres, los	*los padres*	parents
pagar	*pagar*	to pay
página web, la	*la paheena web*	website
páginas amarillas, las	*las paheenas amareeyas*	yellow pages
país, el	*el pays*	country
palabra, la	*la palabra*	word
papel de escribir, el	*el papel de eskreebeer*	writing paper
papel de fumar, el	*el papel de fumar*	cigarette paper
papelería, la	*la papelereea*	stationers'
par, el	*el par*	pair
para	*para*	for
parada de autobús, la	*la parada de awtoboos*	bus stop
parada de taxis, la	*la parada de taksees*	taxi rank
paraguas, el	*el paragwas*	umbrella
parar	*parar*	to stop
parque, el	*el parke*	park
pasaporte, el	*el pasaporte*	passport

paso de cebra, el	el _paso de thebra_	zebra crossing
peaje, el	el _peahe_	toll
pedir	_pedeer_	to order

película, la	_la peleecoola_	**film (cinema)**

San Sebastián, a pituresque coastal town in the Basque Country, hosts Spain's most important film festival every year.

peligro, el	el _peleegro_	danger
pelo, el	el _pelo_	hair
peluquería, la	la _pelookereea_	hairdressers'
pensar	_pensar_	to think
peor	_peor_	worse
pequeño/a	_pekenyo/a_	small
perder	_perder_	to lose
perder (a train)	_perder_	to miss
periódico, el	el _peryodeeko_	newspaper
permiso de conducir, el	el _permeeso de kondootheer_	driving licence
pero	_pero_	but
persona, la	la _persona_	person
personal	_personal_	staff
picadura de mosquito, la	la _peekadoora de moskeeto_	mosquito bite
piscina, la	la _peestheena_	swimming pool
pista de tenis, la	la _peesta de tenees_	tennis court
plano, el (city)	el _plano_	map
playa, la	la _playa_	beach
playa nudista, la	la _playa noodeesta_	nudist beach
poco, un	oon _poko_	a bit
poder	_poder_	to be able
policía, la	la _poleetheea_	police
poner	_poner_	to put
poner en marcha (car)	_poner en marcha_	to start
ponerse en contacto	_ponerse en kontakto_	to contact
por (place)	_por_	by (via)
por (time)	_por_	for
por fin	_por pheen_	at last
por la noche	_por la noche_	overnight
¿por qué?	_por keh?_	why?
porque	_porkeh_	because
posible	_poseeble_	possible
precio, el	el _prethyo_	charge
preferir	_prefeereer_	to prefer

prefijo, el	_el prepheeho_	**area code**

The main prefixes are 91 for Madrid, 93 for Barcelona, 96 for Valencia, 95 for Málaga, 928 for Gran Canaria and 971 for the Balearic islands.

pregunta, la	la _pregoonta_	question
preguntar	_pregoontar_	to ask
preocupado/a	_preokoopado/a_	worried

primeros auxilios, los	*los preemeros awk-seelyos*	first aid
principal	*preentheepal*	main
privado/a	*preebado/a*	private
probablemente	*probablemente*	probably
probador, el	*el probador*	fitting room
problema, el	*el problema*	problem
pronto	*pronto*	soon
propina, la (money)	*la propeena*	tip
pub, el	*el poob*	pub
puerto, el (sea)	*el pwerto*	port
puro, el	*el puro*	cigar

Q

¿qué?	*keh?*	what?
quemar	*kemar*	to burn
querer	*kerer*	to want
¿quién?	*kyen?*	who?
quiosco, el	*el kyosko*	kiosk
quizás	*keethas*	maybe

R

radio, la	*la radyo*	radio
radiografía, la	*la radyographeea*	x-ray
rápido/a (train)	*rapeedo/a*	express
rápido/a	*rapeedo/a*	fast
rayos X, los	*los rayos ekees*	x-rays
real	*real*	real
recado, el	*el rekado*	message
recepción, la	*la rethepthyon*	reception
recepcionista, el/la	*el/la rethepthy-oneesta*	receptionist
receta, la	*la retheta*	prescription
recibir	*retheebeer*	to receive
recibo, el	*el retheebo*	receipt
reclamación, la	*la reklamathyon*	complaint
reclamar	*reklamar*	to complain
recomendar	*rekomendar*	to recommend
recto/a	*rekto/a*	straight
reembolso, el	*el re-embolso*	refund
registrarse (hotel)	*reheestrarse*	to check in
relajarse	*relaharse*	to relax
reloj, el	*el reloh*	watch
reserva, la	*la reserba*	reservation
reservar	*reserbar*	to reserve
responder	*responder*	to answer
retrasado/a	*retrasado/a*	delayed
retraso, el	*el retraso*	delay
reunión, la	*la reoonyon*	meeting
rico/a	*reeko/a*	rich
robar	*robar*	to rob
robo, el	*el robo*	theft
ropa, la	*la ropa*	clothes
ropa interior, la	*la ropa eenteryor*	underwear
ruinas, las	*las rooeenas*	ruins

ruta, la	la *roota*	route

S

saber (knowledge)	*saber*	to know
sala de espera, la	la *sala* de *espera*	waiting room
sala de fiestas, la	la *sala* de *fyestas*	nightclub
salida, la	la *saleeda*	way out
salida de incendios, la	la *saleeda* de een-*thend*yos	fire exit
salir	*saleer*	to leave
sauna, la	la *saona*	sauna
sedante, el	el *sedante*	sedative
sediento/a	*sedyento*/a	thirsty
seguro, el	*esegooro*	insurance
seguro/a	el *segooro*/a	safe
sello, el	el *seyo*	stamp

semana, la	**la se*mana***	**week**

The week before Easter, the **Semana Santa**, is celebrated with spectacular processions all over Catholic Spain.

señal, la	la sen*yal*	sign
señor, el	el *senyor*	sir
señora, la	la sen*yora*	lady
sensato/a	sen*sato*/a	sensible
septiembre	se*tyembre*	September
ser / estar	ser / e*star*	to be
servicio, el	el ser*beethyo*	service
servicio, el (bathroom)	el ser*beethyo*	toilet
servicios de caballeros, los	los ser*beethyos* de kaba*yeros*	gents toilets
servicios de señoras, los	los ser*beethyos* de sen*yoras*	ladies toilets
servir	ser*beer*	to serve
sí	see	yes
SIDA, el	el *seeda*	AIDS
siguiente, el/la	el/la see*gyente*	next
silla de ruedas, la	sa *seeya* de roo*edas*	wheelchair
simpático/a (people)	seem*pateeko*/a	nice
sin	seen	without
síntoma, el	el *seentoma*	symptom
sobre	*sobre*	concerning
socorrista, el/la	el/la sokor*reesta*	lifeguard
¡socorro!	so*korro*	help!
sol, el	el sol	sun
sólo	*solo*	only
somnífero, el	el som*neephero*	sleeping pill
su/s (formal)	*soo*/s	your
suave	soo*abe*	soft
sucio/a	*soothyo*/a	dirty
Sudáfrica	sooda*phreeka*	South Africa
sudafricano/a	sooda*phreekano*/a	South African
sur, el	el *soor*	south

tabaco, el	*el tabako*	tobacco
también	*tambyen*	too
tampones, los	*los tampones*	tampons
taquilla, la	*la takeeya*	box office
tarde	*tarde*	late
tarjeta de crédito, la	*la tarhetta de kredeeto*	credit card
tarjeta de embarque, la	*la tarhetta de embarkeh*	boarding card
taxi, el	*el taksee*	taxi
teclado, el	*el teklado*	keyboard
telefonista, el/la	*el/la telephoneesta*	operator
teléfono, el	*el telephono*	phone
teléfono móvil, el	*el telephono mobil*	mobile phone
televisión, la	*la telebeesyon*	television
temprano	*temprano*	early
tener	*tener*	to have

tener hambre	*tener ambre*	**to be hungry**

You can't go hungry in Spain. There's always a lively **tapas** bars or an inviting restaurants around the corner.

tener que	*tener ke*	must
tener razón	*tener rathon*	to be right
tenis, el	*el tenees*	tennis
terminar	*termeenar*	to finish
terraza, la	*la terratha*	terrace
tiempo, el	*el tyempo*	time, weather
tienda, la	*la tyenda*	shop
tintorería, la	*la teentorereea*	dry cleaners'
típico/a	*teepeeko/a*	typical
todavía	*todabeea*	yet
todo/a (s)	*todo/a(s)*	all
tomar	*tomar*	to take
trabajar (person)	*trabahar*	to work
trabajo, el	*el trabaho*	work
traducir	*tradootheer*	to translate
tranquilo/a	*trankeelo/a*	quiet
transporte público, el	*el transporte poobleeko*	public transport
tranvía, el	*el trambeea*	tram
tren, el	*el tren*	train
triste	*treeste*	sad
tú (informal)	*too*	you
tu/s (informal)	*too/s*	your

úlcera, la	*la oolthera*	ulcer
último/a, el/la	*el/la oolteemo/a*	last
un/a	*oon/a*	a(n)
una vez	*oona beth*	once
urgencias	*oorhentheeas*	A&E
urgente (mail)	*oorhente*	express
urgente	*oorhente*	urgent
usar	*oosar*	to use

usted (formal)	*oos<u>teth</u>*	you
útil	*<u>oo</u>teel*	useful

V

vacaciones, las	*las baka<u>thy</u>ones*	holidays
vacuna, la	*la ba<u>koo</u>na*	vaccine
válido/a	*<u>ba</u>leedo/a*	valid
valor, el	*el ba<u>lor</u>*	value

vegetariano/a	*behetar<u>ya</u>no/a*	**vegetarian**

Vegetarian food is still a bit of a rarity in Spain. Most meals are based on meat.

vehículo, el	*el be<u>hee</u>koolo*	vehicle
velero, el	*el be<u>le</u>ro*	sailing boat
velocidad, la	*la belothee<u>dath</u>*	speed
vender	*ben<u>der</u>*	to sell
venir	*be<u>neer</u>*	to come
verdadero/a	*berda<u>de</u>ro/a*	true
viaje, el	*el by<u>a</u>he*	journey
violación, la	*la beeola<u>thyon</u>*	rape
visado, el	*el bee<u>sa</u>do*	visa
visita, la	*la bee<u>see</u>ta*	visit
visitar	*beesee<u>tar</u>*	to visit
vitamina, la	*la beeta<u>mee</u>na*	vitamin
vomitar	*bomee<u>tar</u>*	to vomit
vuelo, el	*el boo<u>e</u>lo*	flight

W

windsurf	*<u>ween</u>soorph*	windsurfing

X

xenofobia, la	*la ksenopho<u>bee</u>a*	xenophobia
xenófobo/a	*kse<u>no</u>phobo/a*	xenophobe

Y

y	*ee*	and
yate, el	*el <u>ya</u>te*	yacht
yogur, el		yoghurt

Z

zona, la	*la <u>tho</u>na*	zone
zoo, el	*el tho*	zoo

Numbers

0	**cero**	_thero_
1	**uno**	_oono_
2	**dos**	_dos_
3	**tres**	_tres_
4	**cuatro**	_kwatro_
5	**cinco**	_theenko_
6	**seis**	_says_
7	**siete**	_syeteh_
8	**ocho**	_ocho_
9	**nueve**	_nooebeh_
10	**diez**	_dyeth_
11	**once**	_ontheh_
12	**doce**	_dotheh_
13	**trece**	_tretheh_
14	**catorce**	_katortheh_
15	**quince**	_keentheh_
16	**dieciséis**	_dyetheesays_
17	**diecisiete**	_dyetheesyete_
18	**dieciocho**	_dyetheeocho_
19	**diecinueve**	_dyetheenooebe_
20	**veinte**	_bente_
21	**veintiuno**	_benteeuno_
30	**treinta**	_trenta_
40	**cuarenta**	_kwarenta_
50	**cincuenta**	_theenkwenta_
60	**sesenta**	_sesenta_
70	**setenta**	_setenta_
80	**ochenta**	_ochenta_
90	**noventa**	_nobenta_
100	**cien**	_thyen_
1000	**mil**	_meel_
1st	**El/la primero/a**	_el/la preemero/a_
2nd	**El/la segundo/a**	_el/la segundo/a_
3rd	**El/la tercero/a**	_el/la terthero/a_
4th	**El/la cuarto/a**	_el/la kwarto/a_
5th	**El/la quinto/a**	_el/la keento/a_

Weights & measures

English	Spanish	Pronunciation
gram (=0.03oz)	El gramo	el _gramo_
kilogram (=2.2lb)	El kilogramo	el keelo_gramo_
centimetre (=0.4in)	El centímetro	el then_tee_metro
metre (=1.1yd)	El metro	el _metro_
kilometre (=0.6m)	El kilómetro	el kee_lo_metro
litre (=2.1pt)	El litro	el _leetro_

Days & time

English	Spanish	Pronunciation
Monday	El lunes	el _loones_
Tuesday	El martes	el _martes_
Wednesday	El miércoles	el _myer_koles
Thursday	El jueves	el hoo_e_bes
Friday	El viernes	el _byer_nes
Saturday	El sábado	el _sabado_
Sunday	El domingo	el do_meen_go

English	Spanish	Pronunciation
What time is it?	¿Qué hora es?	keh _orah_ es?
(Four) o'clock	Son (las cuatro) en punto	son (las _kwa_tro) en _poon_to
Quarter past/to (six)	Son (las seis) y/menos cuarto	son (las says) ee/menos _kwar_to
Half past (eight)	Son (las ocho) y media	son (las _ocho_) ee _med_ya
morning	La mañana	la man_ya_na
afternoon/evening	La tarde	la _tarde_
night	La noche	la _noche_

Clothes size conversions

Women's clothes	34	36	38	40	42	44	46	50
equiv. UK size	6	8	10	12	14	16	18	20

Men's jackets	44	46	48	50	52	54	56	58
equiv. UK size	34	36	38	40	42	44	46	48

Men's shirts	36	37	38	39	40	41	42	43
equiv. UK size	14	14.5	15	15.5	16	16.5	17	17.5

Shoes	36/37	37/38	39	40	41/42	42/43	44	45
equiv. UK size	4	5	6	7	8	9	10	11